WORDSWORTH
and his world

WORDSWORTH

and his world

BY F. E. HALLIDAY

A STUDIO BOOK

THE VIKING PRESS · NEW YORK

To the memory of Herbert Read

Published in 1970 by The Viking Press, Inc.
625 Madison Avenue, New York, N.Y. 10022

SBN 670–78256–4

Library of Congress catalog card number: 72–84007

Printed and bound in Great Britain by Jarrold and Sons Ltd Norwich

FOREWORD

I cannot have been more than nine years old when, shortly before the First World War, my form-master set me to learn *The Reverie of Poor Susan*. From that moment I was a Wordsworthian, for, like Susan, I too lived in a big city, and her vision inspired in me a corresponding one of mountains, meadows, trees, and rivers that flowed through the sterile streets, a vision that I have never forgotten.

With my parents, I was one of the first to invade the Lake District by car; then, after further schooldays on the fringe of Wordsworth's country, after Cambridge, Wordsworth's university, I returned as a young man to walk the hills and climb the mountains of his poems, in which, like John Stuart Mill a century before me, 'I seemed to draw from a source of inward joy'.

For this is the peculiar glory of Wordsworth's poetry, his early poetry: its consolatory and healing power, its communication of the joy that is to be found in Nature, both in its presence and in its recollection. Never has its message been more important than it is today.

St Ives   F.E.H.
Cornwall

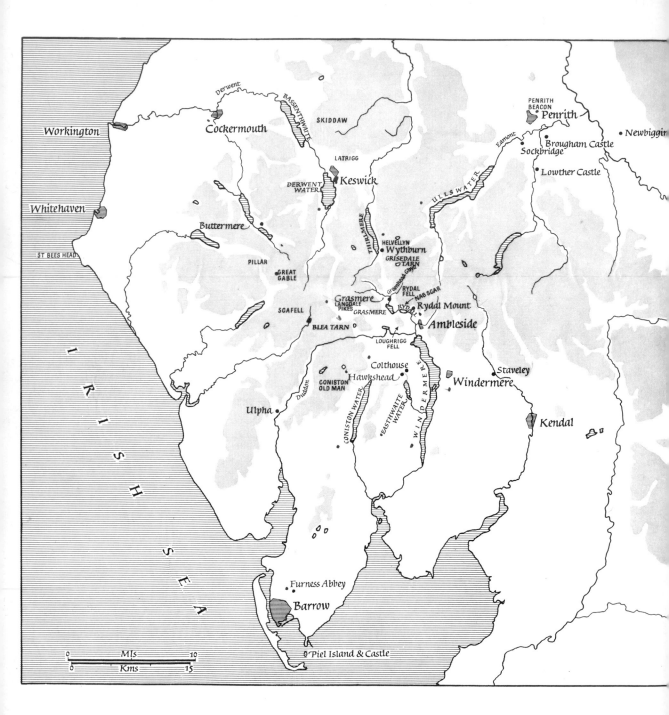

Map of the Lake District

Penrith, Cumberland, where Wordsworth's parents came from, and he himself spent much of his childhood

WHEN JOHN WORDSWORTH married Anne Cookson in 1766, George III was still a popular young sovereign, though just about to embark on the policy that was soon to lead to the American War of Independence and loss of the first British Empire. It was the climax of the classical age in Britain: the age of Robert Adam in architecture, of Sir Joshua Reynolds in painting, and in literature of Dr Johnson, then at the height of his powers. Yet change was in the air: the beginnings of a revolt against the tyranny of rules and reason, the demand for a greater freedom of imagination, an interest in the Middle Ages and mystery, in 'Gothick' and the supernatural; above all, a new appreciation of Nature: not the tame gentlemanly scene of private parks, but Nature wild and solitary. And there were signs of an even more momentous revolution: the invention of machines which, driven by water-power or the new steam-engine, made cotton-spinning in factories far more efficient and economical than by hand in the home. Thus, the boy destined to become the first great romantic poet, of a return to Nature from the town, was born at the beginning of an anti-romantic revolution that sucked country-dwellers out of their fields and villages into hideously spreading industrial towns.

'I was born at Cockermouth, in Cumberland, on April 7th, 1770, the second son of John Wordsworth . . . law-agent to Sir James Lowther.' Wordsworth's birthplace

Birth   The Wordsworths were an old Yorkshire family, though John had been born at Sockbridge, near Penrith, and at the time of his marriage was an able young solicitor who had recently been appointed agent to Sir James Lowther, owner of great estates in Cumberland. His bride, a girl of eighteen, also came from Penrith, the daughter of William Cookson, a mercer, and Dorothy Crackanthorpe of Newbiggin Hall, some eight miles east of the town. As Sir James had bought a house in Cockermouth for his agent, it was there that the young couple made their home, and that their five children were born: Richard in 1768, William on

Sir James Lowther,
first Earl of Lonsdale (1736–1802)

7 April 1770, Dorothy on Christmas Day 1771, John in 1772, and Christopher
in 1774. The eldest and youngest went their own ways, Richard becoming a
London solicitor, and Christopher achieving distinction as Master of Trinity
College, Cambridge; but the three middle children were closely bound in
affection until the set was broken by John's tragic death when only thirty-two.

Perhaps no other decade in English history has been so prolific of genius as the
1770s, for within those ten years, in addition to William Wordsworth, were born
Scott, Coleridge, Southey, Lamb, Landor, Jane Austen, Hazlitt, Turner,

Constable, and Humphry Davy: some compensation for the impending horrors of the Industrial Revolution.

Childhood   The Wordsworth children were fortunate in their birthplace on the northern fringe of the Lake District, a large eighteenth-century house, past the garden of which flowed the River Derwent, mirroring the ruined walls of Cockermouth Castle; and William was never to forget the river's murmur that blended with his nurse's song, and gave him 'a foretaste of the calm that Nature breathes'.

Not far away, at Whitehaven, lived their uncle Richard Wordsworth, where they became acquainted with the sea, ships, and the strange creatures and objects to be found along the shore. But more frequent and prolonged were their visits to their Cookson grandparents at Penrith, an unsympathetic couple, with whose son Christopher, 'Uncle Kit', William never got on. However, he was happy at the village school that he attended in Penrith, where little Mary Hutchinson, 'a phantom of delight', was another pupil.

In his autobiographical poem, *The Prelude*, Wordsworth described the joys of his childhood; how, when only five, he would bathe all a summer's day in a backwater of the river at the bottom of the garden, leap through fields of yellow ragwort, and revel naked in a thunder shower. His sister Dorothy was his constant companion, and together they explored the castle ruins, looked for flowers and birds' nests, and chased butterflies, though the sensitive little girl would not touch them, for fear of brushing the dust off their wings. William was a normal, high-spirited boy, revelling in 'glad animal movements', and it was Dorothy who checked his thoughtless actions:

> *The blessing of my later years*
> *Was with me when a boy:*
> *She gave me eyes, she gave me ears;*
> *And humble cares, and delicate fears;*
> *A heart, the fountain of sweet tears;*
>   *And love, and thought, and joy.*

He can scarcely have remembered his mother, who died shortly before he was eight. However, he heard that she once confessed to a friend that he was the only one of her children about whose future she felt any anxiety. This, he said, was because he was 'of a stiff, moody and violent temper', and gave as an instance his deliberate slashing of a portrait in his grandparents' drawing-room. There followed months of desolation, for his father never recovered his spirits after his wife's death; the boys spent more of their time in the uncongenial Penrith household, and Dorothy was sent to live with relations in Halifax. It was to be nine years before William saw his sister again.

Cockermouth Castle: 'A shattered monument of feudal sway'

Whitehaven, where Wordsworth's uncle Richard was Collector of Customs

'That beloved Vale to which erelong / We were transplanted.' Esthwaite Water, looking towards Hawkshead

(*Above right*) Anne Tyson's cottage, where Wordsworth and his brothers were boarders

(*Left*) 'Hawkshead's happy roof.' The Grammar School that Wordsworth attended, 1779–87

This unhappy period did not last long, for in 1779 William and his elder brother Richard were sent as boarders to Hawkshead Grammar School. Hawkshead is a large village at the head of Esthwaite Water, among the gentler hills of the southern Lake District, between Windermere and Coniston. The school was an Elizabethan foundation, and a good one, and for much of the time he was there William was fortunate in having as his headmaster a young man, William Taylor, who encouraged him to read and try to write poetry. There were about a hundred boys, most of whom boarded with the headmaster, but the Wordsworth boys, all of whom attended the school as they grew old enough, lived with the kindly Anne Tyson in her cottage in the neighbouring hamlet of Colthouse.

William's schooldays at Hawkshead were as happy as his childhood had been at Cockermouth. One of 'a noisy crew', he climbed crags in search of ravens' nests, flew kites from the tops of hills, went fishing in stream and pool, and in winter skated, playing hare and hounds on the frozen lake. In the evenings, by Anne Tyson's warm peat-fire, they would play loo, whist, or other games. As they grew older, they ranged farther afield, racing one another in boats on Windermere, playing bowls at a tavern on its bank, where they feasted on strawberries and cream, and, when they could afford it, hiring horses on which they explored the country as far south as Furness Abbey. Sometimes, however, William's pleasures were solitary, as when half the night – he always loved walking by night – he ranged the hills to set traps for woodcock, or, in early morning before school, rambled round the five miles of Esthwaite Lake, or, when skating, glanced sideway from the throng and, leaning back upon his heels, watched the shadowy banks and solitary cliffs wheel by him.

A change was taking place in the boy. Until adolescence, his happiness had been little more than the physical joy of being alive and healthy, free to roam the hills and exult in sun and wind. But 'those incidental charms', the sports that first attached him to the mountains, lakes and streams, were growing weaker, and he was beginning to love Nature for her own sake. We can see the change taking place in his poem *Nutting*: how one day he set out with his crook, and found a hazel-copse whose milk-white clusters hung inviolate; then, after gloating over his find, he dragged the boughs to earth and rifled them, as so often he had done before. This time, however, as he turned away he felt a sense of guilt, 'a sense of pain when I beheld / The silent trees and saw the intruding sky'.

Perhaps the change was hastened by his father's death, which occurred during the Christmas holidays of 1783, shortly before William's fourteenth birthday. He can have seen but little of his father after he went away to school, for there were only two holidays a year, and John Wordsworth was often away on Lowther business. Yet he had not been without important influence on the boy's development, for he persuaded him to learn passages from Shakespeare, Milton and

◀ Furness Abbey:

*a mouldering pile with fractured arch,
Belfry and images, and living trees.*

'The piercing eye, the thoughtful brow.'
Robert Burns (1759–96)

Spenser, and encouraged him to read. The boy's taste was for fairy-tale and romance, and at home he devoured the *Arabian Nights*, Percy's *Reliques*, *Gulliver's Travels*, *Don Quixote*, *Gil Blas*, and even the novels of Fielding – strong meat for a small boy. But these Cockermouth delights were now over; he was an orphan without a home, almost without money to pay for his further education, though Sir James Lowther owed his father's estate, and therefore the five children, nearly £5000, a debt that was not to be paid for twenty years. Their guardians were their uncles, Richard Wordsworth and Christopher Cookson, and the boys were to spend their Christmas holidays with the one at Whitehaven, their summer holidays with the other in their grandparents' home at Penrith.

For the greater part of the next four years, however, William was at school in his beloved vale of Esthwaite, where old Anne Tyson was a second mother, and his young headmaster a second father. It was probably Taylor who introduced him to contemporary poetry, notably that of James Beattie, whose faith in the beneficent influence of Nature, the joy and love that it imparts, he eagerly accepted, and 'joy' and 'love' were to be the most characteristic words, the very essence, of his own poetry. He himself was beginning to feel a communion with Nature, as though external things were part of his own immaterial being, and sometimes when going to school he had to grasp at a wall or tree to recall himself to reality. George Crabbe's recently published verse tales of the sufferings of the poor also served to recall him to reality, and helped to develop his interest in the lonely pedlars and beggars who wandered about his lakeland countryside. Even more important was the poetry of Burns, with its delight in humble forms of life and ordinary, erring humanity.

'In the month of October, 1787, I was sent to St John's College, Cambridge, of which my uncle, Dr Cookson, had been a fellow'

Wordsworth's room, overlooking Trinity College Chapel, through a window of which he could see Roubiliac's statue of Newton:

The marble index of a mind for ever
Voyaging through strange seas of Thought, alone.

As Penrith was several days' journey from Cambridge, it was June 1788 before he returned, though even then not directly. After exploring Dovedale, he made for Hawkshead and Anne Tyson's cottage, where he stayed for two months. He had left Esthwaite 'a wild, unworldly-minded youth', but returned a sophisticated young man with fashionable clothes and powdered hair, eager to take part in the revelry of Windermere and its neighbourhood. One magnificent morning, however, as he walked back to Hawkshead after a night of dancing, the beauty of the sunrise was a revelation that convinced him of his true vocation:

> *My heart was full; I made no vows, but vows*
> *Were then made for me; bond unknown to me*
> *Was given, that I should be, else sinning greatly,*
> *A dedicated Spirit.*

Again, some weeks later, when walking home by moonlight after another night of 'strenuous idleness', he met an emaciated soldier whose tale of hardship so moved him to pity that he took him to a cottage to be cared for. He now knew that he

> *That streamlet whose blue current works its way*
> *Between romantic Dovedale's spiry rocks.*

A Cumberland lead mine

was destined to be a poet, and that his theme was not Nature only, but humanity, the humble men and women of his remote countryside. Accompanied by an old friend, Anne Tyson's terrier, he began to compose *An Evening Walk* as he 'sauntered, like a river running / And talking to itself', a favourite mode of composition that was to earn him a reputation for something more than eccentricity: 'He goes bumming and muffling, and talking to hissen,' a neighbour once remarked, 'but *whiles* he's as sensible as you or me!'

In Penrith he resumed his rambles with Dorothy and Mary Hutchinson, but he thought of Philip Sidney, who wrote the *Arcadia* for his sister, and it was for Dorothy, 'my dearest friend', not Mary, that he wrote *An Evening Walk*. In conventional heroic couplets, overloaded with adjectives, he celebrated Esthwaite, Rydal and Grasmere, and described the occupations of the natives: potters with their panniered horses, peasants with their sledges, timber-wains groaning down the mountainside, boat-builders by the water's edge, and the muffled thunder of blasting in slate quarries. Significantly, the most original, and memorable, passage is the story that he inserted of a wandering woman whose husband has been killed in the American War, and whose children die of cold and hunger in her arms. The poem finishes with a vision of the moonlight gilding the cottage where he and Dorothy 'to golden days shall rise'.

He returned to Cambridge in October, and in the following month Dorothy, 'almost mad with joy', escaped from Penrith and her Uncle Kit, and went to

live with his younger brother William and his newly married wife at Forncett Rectory near Norwich, only fifty miles from Cambridge. They visited him on their way to their new home, and Dorothy was enchanted by all that she saw in Cambridge.

William Cookson was a Fellow of St John's with plans for his needy nephew's future; he was to follow in his footsteps: a fellowship, ordination, and a college living. William was prepared to consider ordination, but instead of reading mathematics for a fellowship, he devoted himself almost entirely to the poets, not only the classics, but English poets, from Chaucer to Collins and Cowper, and even Italian, none of whom had anything to do with the course for his degree, which, when he took it, was merely a B A without honours.

French Revolution　It was shortly after visiting Dorothy and the Cooksons at Forncett in the summer of 1789 that he heard of the fall of the Bastille, the Paris prison that was the hateful symbol of feudal tyranny in France. Frenchmen had helped the American colonists to gain their independence, and now the Paris mob was asserting its right to similar liberties. A new age had begun.

The news seems to have made little impression on Wordsworth, an inexperienced boy of nineteen with little interest in politics, but in the following year he decided to go on a walking-tour through France to the romantic scenery of Switzerland. His companion was a college friend, Robert Jones, a short, plump Welshman, an odd contrast to the tall, gaunt dalesman, who confessed to Dorothy that their appearance often raised smiles as they strode along with oak-sticks in their hands and bundles on their heads.

Walking-Tour in France　They sailed from Dover on 13 July 1790, and in Calais found the people celebrating the day of Louis XVI's oath of fidelity to the new Constitution.

Wordsworth was probably staying with Dorothy and their uncle William Cookson at Forncett Rectory (*left*) when the French Revolution began with the storming of the Bastille, 14 July 1789 (*above*)

Rejoicing in Paris, July 1790, when Wordsworth and Robert Jones landed in France

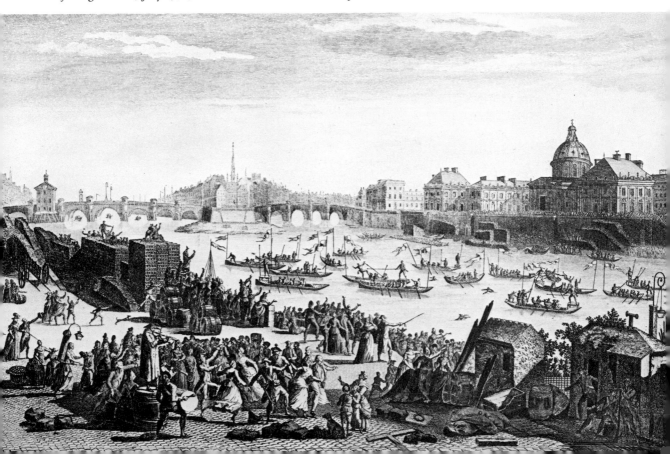

Wordsworth was a prodigious walker, and Jones cannot have found it easy to cover the forty miles a day that he sometimes demanded. Avoiding Paris, they made for Burgundy, and at Châlon sailed down the Saône with a company of Frenchmen rejoicing in their new liberties and, 'with flowing cups elate', danced hand in hand with them round the supper table. From Lyons they walked to the monastery of the Grande Chartreuse, and so to Mont Blanc and Chamonix 'With its dumb cataracts and streams of ice'. They crossed the Alps by the Simplon Pass, and walked down into Italy, to Locarno and the Lake of Como, the serene beauty of which Wordsworth always remembered with joy. Indeed, he felt sure at the time that the recollection of all these sights would be a source of future happiness. He never missed a chance of seeing a waterfall, and on their way back they visited Schaffhausen and Lauterbrunnen; then at Basle they bought a small boat and steered themselves down the Rhine – a hazardous undertaking – to Cologne. They walked through Belgium to Calais, and were back in Cambridge by the middle of October. In December William went to Forncett, where he celebrated Dorothy's nineteenth birthday on Christmas Day.

(*Opposite above*) Mer de Glace, Chamonix:
'A motionless array of mighty waves'

Beheld the Convent of Chartreuse, and there
Rested within an awful solitude.

'. . . to Schaffhausen, to view the falls of the Rhine. Magnificent as this fall certainly is, I must confess I was disappointed in it. I had raised my ideas too high'

'Half-rural Sadler's Wells'

He found her very happy, helping with her uncle's parochial duties, and she found him the most affectionate of brothers: 'a sort of violence of Affection', combined with a rare delicacy of manners. The weather was mild, and for hours they paced the garden together planning their future, Dorothy's ideal being a 'little parsonage' where she could keep house for William. But William was undecided; rather than the Church, perhaps the Law, or even the Army; but above all he wanted to be a poet, and after taking his degree in January 1791, he went to London, where he could be alone among the multitude and perhaps make up his mind. He had been there once before, on a short visit, when, as he approached the great city on the roof of the coach, he had suddenly felt the weight of history descend upon his heart, not as an oppression, but as one of his mystical experiences. Ignorant of city life, he came merely as an observer, and was fascinated by the sights of the 'monstrous ant-hill', the

'Siddons in the fulness of her power'

Oh! the beating heart
When one among the prime of these rose up.
Pitt addressing the House of Commons

mystery of the swarms of people, each bent on his own business, each unknown to others, yet each, he felt, part of a great whole. The life of the streets: vendors, ballad-singers, beggars, dissolute men, shameless women and innocent children, was his main interest, yet the theatre was also a dear delight, and he frequented Drury Lane to see Mrs Siddons, and Sadler's Wells to watch the clowns and acrobats. He also attended the Law Courts and House of Commons, where he heard the young Prime Minister, Pitt, speak. It was a critical time in international affairs, for the Paris mob was getting out of hand, and Louis XVI a prisoner in the Tuileries.

Wordsworth's twenty-first birthday passed unnoticed in the obscurity of London, but at the end of May he went to North Wales to stay with Robert Jones at his

London

Wales home near Ruthin. The two friends resumed their walking, visited Anglesey, the winding Dee, 'the Alpine steeps of the Conway', and climbed Snowdon on a night of dripping fog. There Wordsworth had another visitation when, on nearing the summit, he found himself in bright moonlight, a sea of mist below, broken by a dark abyss from which appeared to come the roar of waters: symbol of a majestic intellect, 'emblem of a mind / That feeds upon infinity'.

Not unreasonably, the guardians who had financed his education were pressing him to decide on a career, but at this time occurred an event that gave him an excuse for further procrastination. The debt owed to his father by Sir James Lowther, now Earl of Lonsdale, had not been paid, and in August 1791 the case was brought to court at Carlisle. Lord Lonsdale was ordered to pay, and William and his brothers and sister should each have received more than £1000, a capital sum that would mean an income of nearly £100 a year, enough for a frugal bachelor to live on in those days. But the exact sum was left to arbitration, and as Lord Lonsdale was too influential to be hurried, the debt was still outstanding when he died. William, therefore, decided to go to France to learn the language, with the professed intention of obtaining a travelling tutorship on his return, and in November 1791 he sailed from Brighton to Dieppe.

France He stayed a few days in Paris, surveying the scene much as he had surveyed that of London, as a dispassionate observer, wandering round the areas of tavern, gaming-house and brothel; he pocketed a stone from the ruins of the Bastille, but affected more emotion than he felt, and was more deeply moved by Lebrun's painting of the Magdalene. Although his sympathies were with the struggle for liberty, he knew too little about the causes and progress of the Revolution to take sides, and when he moved to Orléans at the beginning of December his companions were royalist officers, counter-revolutionaries who tried to convert him to their cause.

Annette It was probably in the house where he lodged that he met Annette Vallon, a young woman with royalist sympathies, four years older than himself. We know that he had 'a sort of violence of affection', and the youth, for he was little more, was quite carried away by his passion, for in April, when Annette returned to her home in Blois, she was pregnant. William followed, no doubt intending to marry her, for he made up his mind to be ordained on his return to England; he had to have some profession to support her, though what his parishioners would make of his Catholic wife would be a disturbing thought.

I westward took my way, to see the sun
Rise, from the top of Snowdon.

'France lured me forth.' Dieppe, where Wordsworth landed on his momentous, second visit, 28 November 1791

'Tavern, Brothel, Gaming-house and Shop.'
Paris in 1791: a roulette game (*left*) and a street
scene of Savoyards with performing dogs (*below*)

These various sights . . .
Appeared to recompense the traveller's pains
Less than the painted Magdalene of Le Brun.

31

Beaupuy   He must at this time have been in a highly emotional state, an almost penniless young man in a strange country involved in revolution, and passionately in love with a girl who would soon bear him a child. And it was now, soon after his arrival in Blois, that he met an officer very different from those with whom he had so far associated: Michel Beaupuy, a man of thirty-five and noble birth, yet a passionate supporter of the Revolution. Wordsworth tells us that he was twenty-two when he came to rank Man in his affections on an equality with Nature,

Annette Vallon:
a reputed portrait

Beaupuy - let the name
Stand near the worthiest of Antiquity!

(*Opposite above*)
Orleans, *a pleasant town*
Washed by the current of the stately Loire.

and it was Beaupuy to whom he owed this new allegiance. He loved man as man, regardless of social standing; and while discussing liberty and the rights of man on one of their many walks, angrily exclaimed, 'It is against *that* that we are fighting,' as they passed a hungry girl leading a starving heifer. Beaupuy was one of the main influences in Wordsworth's life, for though their companionship lasted only a few months, until July 1792, he converted him into a 'patriot' like himself, a revolutionary republican.

> *Bliss was it in that dawn to be alive,*
> *But to be young was very heaven!*

That, however, was written in retrospect, and 'in that dawn', however much he may have valued Beaupuy's friendship and adored Annette, bliss must have been tempered with anxiety. No doubt he hoped that the Vallon family would accept the situation when they discovered Annette's condition, but if so, he was disappointed, for in September she was sent back to Orléans. Again Wordsworth followed, and there wrote *Descriptive Sketches*, a despondent account of his joyous

◀ Blois, the fateful town where Annette Vallon lived, and Wordsworth met Beaupuy

walking-tour through France two years before. It might earn him a few pounds if published, and at the end of October he left Annette, presumably to make preparations for her reception in England.

Paris, however, gave him pause. It was very different from the city he had left nearly a year before. France was now a republic at war with Austria, and Paris in the hands of the extremists of the Jacobin Party: Danton, Marat, Robespierre. In September, shortly before his arrival, the mob had massacred hundreds of suspected royalists, and the Reign of Terror had begun. Taught by Beaupuy, who believed that revolutionary changes could be achieved without bloodshed, by reason and persuasion, Wordsworth was a republican; but mob violence sickened him, and he gloomily wondered what would be the outcome of this new tyranny, and even considered helping the moderate Girondin Party. But his funds were exhausted, and he returned to London to raise more. He arrived at about the time his daughter Caroline was born in Orléans, on 15 December 1792.

First publications

He stayed with his elder brother Richard, the businessman and legal adviser of the family, probably in the hope of raising money for a speedy return to Annette. For the same reason he hurried his two poems through the press, *An Evening Walk* and *Descriptive Sketches*, but by the time they appeared early in February 1793, England was at war with France. Ten years later he wrote that this was the first great shock to his moral nature: that England should be an ally of the reactionary powers of Europe against the republic of Beaupuy. Certainly he wrote a violent reply (that was not published) to the Bishop of Llandaff's denunciation of republican France and eulogy of British institutions. In his *Letter to the Bishop* he attacked these institutions: the monarchy, aristocracy, judicature, an unrepresentative Parliament, demanded votes for all men, an equal distribution of wealth, and signed himself 'A Republican'.

War with France

The Republican

Yet, to a young man of violent passions, revolution abroad and injustice at home, however deeply felt, mean little in comparison with the loss of the woman he loves. When he came to write *The Prelude*, Wordsworth did not mention the Annette affair, and attributed his anguish at this time to Robespierre, the Reign of Terror and the French war, though it was France that had declared war, not England. There can be little doubt, however, that the real cause of his distress was the loss of Annette and Caroline, whom, but for the war, but for his delay, he might have brought to England; and in the autumn he seems to have got as far as Paris in a desperate attempt to see them.

Execution of Louis XVI, 21 January 1793

Robespierre, who 'Wielded the sceptre of the Atheist crew', is wounded

His movements in these critical years of despondency, 1793–95, are sometimes difficult to trace. Dorothy, to whom he would have flown for comfort, was almost as inaccessible in Forncett as Annette in Blois. His uncle William would not receive an unmarried father and republican who had advocated the confiscation of the wealth of the French Church, still less help him towards ordination and a benefice. Fortunately he came across an old schoolfellow of some means, William Calvert, who offered to take him on a tour in the west of England, and he gratefully accepted. In July they were in the Isle of Wight, where Wordsworth gazed towards France, and gloomily watched the British fleet assembling, but on Salisbury Plain an accident to their carriage put an end to their tour. Calvert rode north, and Wordsworth pursued his way on foot to Bristol, up the Wye Valley, past Tintern, to the home of Robert Jones, where he stayed and wrote *Salisbury Plain*, the later title of which, *Guilt and Sorrow*, indicates his state of mind.

Despondency   He spent Christmas at Whitehaven, and early in 1794 stayed with Calvert and his brother Raisley at Windy Brow, a farmhouse that they owned on the hills above Keswick. As Dorothy was then staying in Halifax, and Calvert offered them the house for a few weeks, William went to fetch her, and in April brother and sister were reunited in their native countryside. Dorothy was overjoyed, but practical, calculating how little they could live on together: 'Our breakfast and supper are of milk, and our dinner chiefly of potatoes, and we drink no tea.' It

Wordsworth's first publication. The 'Young Lady' was his sister Dorothy

A N

EVENING WALK.

An EPISTLE;

In VERSE.

ADDRESSED to a Young LADY,

FROM THE

LAKES

OF THE

NORTH of ENGLAND.

BY

W. WORDSWORTH, B. A.

Of St. JOHN's, CAMBRIDGE.

LONDON:

Printed for J. Johnson, St. Paul's Church-Yard.

1793.

(*Opposite above*)
'Pile of Stonehenge!' The scene of *Guilt and Sorrow*

(*Right*) '"Robespierre is dead!" . . . Great was my transport, deep my gratitude.' July 1794

was a rehearsal for the time when they should live together always in their own cottage.

In May they started on their first walking tour together, passing through Cockermouth, where they saw their birthplace empty and neglected, on their way to visit relations on the coast. There William left Dorothy and returned to Windy Brow, where Raisley Calvert was dying of consumption. Wordsworth, so confident in himself, inspired confidence in others, and so impressed young Calvert that he promised to leave him a legacy, so that he could settle down and write without taking up a profession. Wordsworth stayed with Raisley most of the time until he died in January 1795, when he inherited £900. It was enough for his immediate needs, and he went to London.

'I begin to wish much to be in Town,' he had written from Keswick to his friend William Mathews. 'Cataracts and mountains are good occasional society, but they will not do for constant companions.' It is an astonishing remark from the poet for whom these things were a constant source of joy, and a measure of his distracted mind. Even cataracts and mountains were less important than Annette; he was nearer to her in London than in Keswick, and he now had the money to bring her to England and marry her, as soon as he had the chance. But it was to be another seven years before he had the chance, and then it was too late.

He abandoned the idea of the Church as a profession; it had never appealed to him; he was a deist rather than a believer in Christianity, and ordination would mean tacit support of the British Constitution, of which he disapproved. He considered journalism as a means of publishing his opinions, and wrote: 'I am one of that odious class of men called democrats . . . I disapprove of monarchical and aristocratical governments, however modified.' And he sought comfort in the company and philosophy of William Godwin, the author of *Political Justice*. But Godwin's belief in reason was totally opposed to his own faith in feeling and intuition, and led to such mental conflict that he 'yielded up moral questions in despair'.

Racedown with Dorothy

He was saved from complete collapse by the Cambridge acquaintance with whom he stayed in London: Basil Montagu, a young lawyer and widower with a two-year-old son, another Basil. Montagu introduced him to his friend John Pinney, son of a wealthy merchant who lived in Bristol, and had another, rarely used, house in the country, Racedown Lodge. Like Raisley Calvert, young Pinney was much impressed by Wordsworth, and persuaded his father to let him and Dorothy have Racedown rent-free, provided he and his brother could use it occasionally. At the same time, Montagu offered Wordsworth £50 a year if he and Dorothy would look after little Basil. Wordsworth jumped at the offers, and went to stay with the Pinneys in Bristol to await the arrival of Dorothy from Halifax; by the end of September they and young Basil were at Racedown.

William Godwin (1756–1836), whom
Wordsworth met in February 1795

John F. Pinney, who lent Racedown to
Wordsworth

Their new home was a small country house among the Dorset hills, a few miles
north-east of Lyme Regis. Dorothy's girlhood wish was at last fulfilled: to look
after William, if not in a Cumberland cottage, at least in a house among hills
that reminded her of her 'native wilds', and she did her best to comfort her brother:

> *She whispered still that brightness would return;*
> *She, in the midst of all, preserved me still*
> *A Poet, made me seek beneath that name,*
> *And that alone, my office upon earth.*

They walked, and gardened, and read together, and there was little Basil, 'a
charming boy', to entertain them.

They were lonely, however, and William remained unhappy, in spite of
Dorothy, in spite of release from immediate financial anxiety. Indeed, Calvert's
legacy may have aggravated his remorse at having left Annette behind; she and
Caroline might now have been with them at Racedown. Then, the French
Revolution had gone wrong; defence of the republic had become a war of
aggression; revolution had not led to the regeneration, but degeneration of man-
kind; England was threatened with invasion, and a panicky government was
passing repressive laws. He could not write, though he did revise *Salisbury Plain*,
the long, sombre story of poverty, murder, and retribution.

◄ 'I settled with my only sister at Racedown in Dorsetshire,' 26 September 1795

Two new friends of 1795:
Robert Southey (1774–1843).
'He is very pleasant in his
manners, and a man of great
reading, in old books.'

In Bristol he had met two ardent young radicals, Robert Southey, a native of the town, and his friend Samuel Taylor Coleridge, who had recently abandoned their scheme to establish a communistic society, a 'pantisocracy', in America, and married the sisters Edith and Sara Fricker. As Coleridge had read and admired *An Evening Walk* and *Descriptive Sketches*, Wordsworth sent him *Salisbury Plain*, which again he praised for its originality and depth of feeling. Encouraged by this, perhaps, Wordsworth began to write a blank-verse tragedy, *The Borderers*, in which the villain Oswald plays the part of Iago to the Othello of the hero Marmaduke and Lear of Herbert, the aged father of the heroine. And it is the tempter, Oswald, who utters the words that most vividly reveal Wordsworth's anguish at this time:

And Southey's brother-in-law, Samuel Taylor Coleridge (1772–1834): 'A noticeable Man with large grey eyes'

Action is transitory – a step, a blow . . .
Suffering is permanent, obscure and dark,
And shares the nature of infinity.

Oswald was a study of such a man as Robespierre: 'Power is life to him . . . When he cannot govern, he will destroy.' But in the writing of the tragedy Wordsworth appears to have worked off the accumulated pessimism of the last four years, for when it was finished in the spring of 1797 Dorothy wrote: 'Mary Hutchinson is staying with us. She is one of the best girls in the world, and we are as happy as human beings can be, that is when William is at home . . . He is the life of the whole house.'

Mary Hutchinson

Joseph Cottle
(1770–1835),
the Bristol publisher

The cottage at Nether Stowey, where Coleridge lived

Coleridge   Wordsworth had not seen Mary since his affair with Annette, and her serene and happy presence, though in one way disturbing, must have contributed greatly to his recovery that spring. Then, no sooner had Mary gone than Coleridge unexpectedly arrived, shortening his approach by leaping a gate and bounding across a field in his eagerness to reach the house. The arrival of this gay, exuberant young genius was perhaps the most important event in Wordsworth's life. The two poets lost no time. Wordsworth read aloud his new poem, *The Ruined Cottage*, then after tea, Coleridge 'repeated' two and a half acts of his tragedy *Osorio*; and next morning Wordsworth replied with *The Borderers*.

'You had a great loss in not seeing Coleridge,' wrote Dorothy to Mary. 'He is a wonderful man.' And early in July Coleridge wrote to his Bristol friend and publisher Joseph Cottle: 'W. and his exquisite sister are with me. She is a woman indeed! in mind I mean and heart . . . In every motion her most innocent soul outbeams so brightly . . . Her eye watchful in minutest observation of Nature.' As for that 'Giant Wordsworth – God love him!' he was 'a very great man, the only man to whom at all times and in all modes of excellence' Coleridge felt himself inferior. He had been so bewitched by brother and sister that he had persuaded them to repay his visit, and carried them off to his cottage at Nether Stowey near the north coast of Somerset, where they met his wife Sara and baby son Hartley. It was there that Wordsworth first met Charles Lamb, who came to stay with the Coleridges for a few days.

The village of Nether Stowey lies at the foot of the Quantock Hills, and William and Dorothy at once fell in love with the countryside, which reminded them of Cumberland. With their diviner's instinct, for they were always drawn by running water, they found 'a sequestered waterfall' in the grounds of Alfoxden House, three miles west of Stowey, and as it was to be let furnished at a nominal rent, they took it, fetched Basil from Racedown, and by the middle of July were in residence.

'Here we are in a large mansion, in a large park, with seventy head of deer around us,' Dorothy wrote to Mary. The mansion is a handsome Queen Anne country house, immediately in front of which, to the south, rises the steep slope of the Quantocks, studded with fine oaks and crowned with a copse of beeches. To the north, across the intervening woods and meadows, is the sea. Such a house in such a setting, with the companionship and inspiration of Dorothy and Coleridge, a constant visitor, was the ideal place for Wordsworth's spiritual recuperation, and he began to write of other things than guilt and suffering.

Alfoxden House, 'a large mansion, with furniture enough for a dozen families like ours . . .
In front is a little court, with grass plot, gravel walk, and shrubs.' DW to MH, 14 August 1797

In November came the memorable tour when the three – William, Dorothy and Coleridge – set off towards Watchet and Dulverton to make a circuit of the hills. Their expenses were to be defrayed by writing a poem for a magazine, and during the tour the two young poets – Coleridge was only twenty-five – began their collaboration. This was the genesis of *The Ancient Mariner*, the story of which was mainly Coleridge's invention, though Wordsworth made a few suggestions. He had for so long been obsessed by the theme of crime and retribution that it was he who proposed the shooting of the albatross and consequent spectral persecution. He also contributed a few lines, but before their return to Alfoxden he had withdrawn from the venture, feeling that his bent was not for the supernatural, and that his intervention would 'only have been a clog'. Otherwise, he was anything but a clog, and each struck fire from the other. Thanks to Wordsworth, Coleridge was now at the beginning of his short burst of inspired creative activity – he had just written *Kubla Khan* – and he finished the long ballad in the course of the winter.

The Ancient Mariner. 'I also suggested the navigation of the ship by the dead men'

◄ 'We set off, and proceeded along the Quantock Hills, towards Watchet; and in the course of this walk was planned the poem of the *Ancient Mariner*'

Wordsworth, too, was busy: developing *The Ruined Cottage*, which he claimed was to be part of a long philosophical poem to be called *The Recluse: or Views of Nature, Man and Society*. Coleridge had himself contemplated writing such a poem, but, feeling that Wordsworth was better able to express a system of philosophy in verse, had persuaded him to begin the task, a task with which, in spite of Coleridge's repeated exhortations, he was never to make much headway. He was more interested in the coming of spring to Alfoxden and, shortly before his twenty-eighth birthday, wrote:

> *It is the first mild day of March:*
> *Each minute sweeter than before,*
> *The redbreast sings from the tall larch*
> *That stands beside our door.*

The poem was addressed to Dorothy and Coleridge: a lyric in ballad metre. The great creative period had begun, and in the spring and summer of this year, 1798, he wrote the poems that were his contribution to the *Lyrical Ballads*.

Fortunately Dorothy kept a *Journal* of these momentous months: notes that describe not only their doings, but also her own sensitive observation of Nature, sometimes borrowed by her brother and Coleridge for their own ends:

January 20th, 1798. The green paths down the hill-sides are channels for streams. . . . The shafts of the trees show in the light like the columns of a ruin.

31st. Set forward to Stowey at half-past five.

February 3rd. Walked with Coleridge over the hills.

14th. Gathered sticks with William in the wood, he being unwell and not able to go further.

17th. No other sound but that of the water, and the slender notes of a redbreast.

March 7th. William and I drank tea at Coleridge's. A cloudy sky. . . . One only leaf upon the top of a tree – the sole remaining leaf – danced round and round like a rag blown by the wind. [*Christabel*, 49–52.]

9th. A clear sunny morning, went to meet Mr and Mrs Coleridge. The day very warm.

18th. The Coleridges left us. A cold, windy morning. Walked with them half way. On our return, sheltered under the hollies, during a hail-shower. The withered leaves danced with the hailstones. William wrote a description of the storm. ['A whirl-blast from behind the hill.']

19th. Wm. and Basil and I walked to the hill-tops. . . . William wrote some lines describing a stunted thorn. [*The Thorn.*]

23rd. Coleridge dined with us. He brought his ballad finished. . . . A beautiful evening, very starry, the horned moon.

25th. Walked to Coleridge's after tea. Arrived at home at one o'clock. The night cloudy but not dark. [*Christabel*, 15.]

April 1st. Walked by moonlight.

20th. William all the morning engaged in wearisome composition. The moon crescent. *Peter Bell* begun.

26th. William went to have his picture taken.

May 6th, Sunday. Expected the painter, and Coleridge.

Peter Bell, begun exactly a month after Coleridge had shown him the finished *Ancient Mariner*, was Wordsworth's version of the same theme, and his treatment of it was characteristically different; Coleridge had tried to make the supernatural appear natural, but Wordsworth's aim was to make the natural appear supernatural. Then, the poem may have been something more than a story of crime and redemption: the emblem of his own release from remorse at his failure to marry Annette, the admission that his passion was dead. Perhaps that was why it remained so long unpublished.

Dorothy's last entries in her *Journal* were made towards the end of May, when she and William and Coleridge walked to Cheddar, and 'slept at Cross'. The Alfoxden year was almost over. Even at Racedown Wordsworth's eccentricities, his mouthing verses as he walked, his nocturnal rambles, and use of a pocket telescope, had roused suspicions among the Dorset peasants. Now, when the danger of invasion was even greater, the strange goings-on at Alfoxden led to the employment of a government spy: the Wordsworths and their friends carried camp-stools on their excursions, by night as well as by day; they entered observations in a portfolio, which they were overheard to say was almost finished; there was a woman who passed as the sister of one of the men, but she had a suspiciously dark complexion; and they washed and mended their clothes on Sundays. The visit of the notorious 'Citizen John' Thelwall, recently tried for high treason, was the last straw, and the owner refused to renew the lease of Alfoxden after midsummer.

'Coleridge, William, and myself set forward to the Cheddar rocks.' DW, *Journal*, 16 May 1798

William Hazlitt (1778–1830).
'I got into a metaphysical
argument with Wordsworth.'
The two men quarrelled a few
years later

As the Wordsworths would soon be homeless, Coleridge proposed a visit to Germany to learn the language. He and his wife could afford to go, for Thomas and Josiah Wedgwood had just promised him an annuity of £150, but William and Dorothy would have to raise funds. The plan to write a joint poem to defray the expenses of the Dulverton tour had come to nothing, or rather, it had come to very much more: *The Ancient Mariner* and the recent lyrics of Wordsworth. They sent them to Cottle, who agreed to publish them as *Lyrical Ballads* and advanced ten guineas; and William and Dorothy made preparations for Germany.

We have a description of Wordsworth at this time, when William Shuter, an obscure provincial artist, was painting his portrait for Cottle. It is Hazlitt recalling their first meeting in Coleridge's cottage; and Hazlitt knew his subject, for he himself painted Wordsworth's portrait in 1803. 'He answered in some degree to his friend's description of him, but was more gaunt and Don Quixote-like. He was quaintly dressed (according to the costume of that unconstrained period) in a brown fustian jacket and striped pantaloons. There was something of a roll, a lounge in his gait, not unlike his own "Peter Bell". . . . He sat down and talked very naturally and freely, with a mixture of clear gushing accents in his voice, a deep guttural intonation, and a strong tincture of the northern burr, like the crust on wine.' This broad northern accent should be remembered when reading Wordsworth's poetry, in which *thrush* rhymes with *bush*, *note* with *nought*, *road* with *broad*, *flood* with *stood*, *doors* with *wooers*, and *water* with *chatter*.

'William went to have his picture taken.' DW, *Journal*, 26 April 1798. The painter was William Shuter

Wye Valley   Having sent little Basil to live with an aunt, William and Dorothy left Alfoxden at midsummer, and went for a tour of the Wye Valley, up which Wordsworth had walked five years before. They passed, repassed, and returned to sleep at Tintern, and the harvest of their journey was the *Lines Written a Few Miles above Tintern Abbey*. Wordsworth did not write them there, however, but composed them on the way back to Bristol, where he wrote them down and took them to Cottle for inclusion in *Lyrical Ballads*.

'Lyrical Ballads'

The volume, published anonymously in September, began with *The Ancient Mariner* and finished with *Tintern Abbey*, between which were two more poems by Coleridge and twenty by Wordsworth, who also wrote a short 'Advertisement': 'The majority of the following poems are to be considered as experiments. They were written chiefly with a view to ascertain how far the language of conversation in the middle and lower classes of society is adapted to the purposes of poetic pleasure.'

It was a revolutionary manifesto that might almost have been written 120 years later, when T. S. Eliot startled the world with *Prufrock*. The contents were equally revolutionary, extending the range of poetry, preparing the way for the dramatic monologues of Browning and all that followed. Although most readers in 1798 were unable to accept the conversation of the lower classes as poetry, the simplicity

Tintern Abbey:

Five years have passed, five summers, with the length
Of five long winters, and again I hear
These waters rolling from their mountain springs,
With a soft inland murmur.

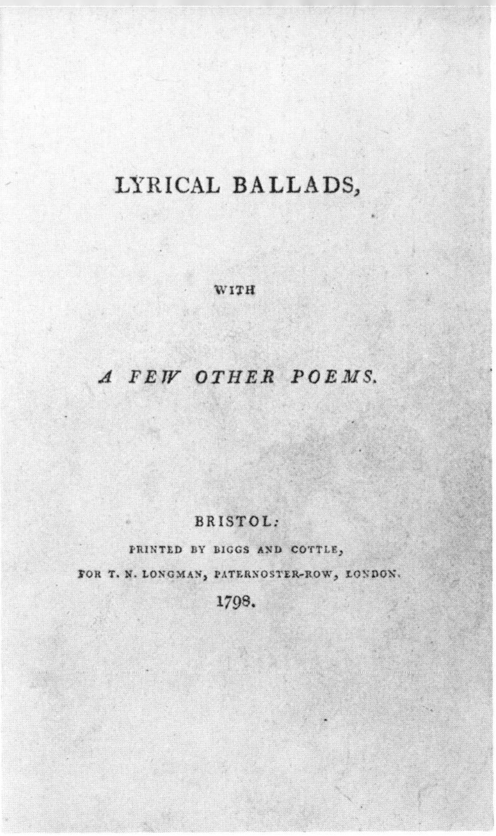

LYRICAL BALLADS,

WITH

A FEW OTHER POEMS.

BRISTOL:
PRINTED BY BIGGS AND COTTLE,
FOR T. N. LONGMAN, PATERNOSTER-ROW, LONDON.
1798.

Lyrical Ballads, title page of the first edition.
'A greater number have been pleased than I
ventured to hope I should please'

and freshness of these lyrics in ballad form put an end to the otiose poetic diction of the day, 'the inane phraseology of many modern writers', as Wordsworth put it, among whom he might have classed the youthful author of his own first published poems. There is a world of difference between the mannered couplets of *An Evening Walk*, with its echoes of Gray's *Elegy*:

Below Eve's listening Star the sheep walk stills
Its drowsy tinklings on th'attentive hills,

and the *Lines Written in Early Spring* beside the waterfall at Alfoxden:

I heard a thousand blended notes,
While in a grove I sate reclined,
In that sweet mood when pleasant thoughts
Bring sad thoughts to the mind;

or *The Tables Turned*, written after an argument with Hazlitt:

One impulse from a vernal wood
May teach you more of man;
Of moral evil and of good,
Than all the sages can.

It is lines like these that we recall when we think of Wordsworth's poetry, lines limpid as a mountain stream, pure as the viol's music.

'The Lyrical Ballads are not esteemed well here,' wrote Sara Coleridge. Nor were they widely noticed, though in the *Critical Review* Southey had some sour things to say about *The Ancient Mariner*, *The Idiot Boy*, *The Thorn*, and 'most of the ballads'; yet, he added, no praise could be too high for the passage in *Tintern Abbey*, beginning, 'Though changed, no doubt, from what I was . . .' Most critics would agree; they are the quintessence of Wordsworth, describing the progress of his relationship with Nature: from the 'animal' enjoyment of boyhood, through the rapturous period inspired only by the senses, when 'The sounding cataract / Haunted me like a passion', to the thoughtful maturity in which he wrote, when to such sights and sounds were added 'the still, sad music of humanity', and intimations of a presence, a spirit, a motion that 'rolls through all things', uniting Man with Nature.

By this time, thanks to the genius of Napoleon, a man of Wordsworth's own age, France was master of much of Europe, including Italy and Switzerland, but after the victory off Cape St Vincent in 1797, Britain was mistress of the seas; and the threat of invasion receded when Napoleon attacked Egypt on his way to occupy India. In August 1798, however, Nelson annihilated his fleet in Aboukir Bay, and it was another year before Napoleon could get back to France.

Germany   Shortly after Nelson's victory 'of the Nile', and shortly before the publication of *Lyrical Ballads*, William, Dorothy and Coleridge, but not Sara, left Bristol for Yarmouth and sailed for Hamburg, 'a *sad* place', where Dorothy began another *Journal*. They met the aged poet Klopstock, any one of whose odes was reputed to be worth all the lyric poetry of England; but Dorothy was disappointed by his lack of sublimity, and they discussed blank verse – in French. That was the trouble;

The Battle of Cape St Vincent, in which
Nelson made his name, 14 February 1797

Goethe (1749–1832). 'I have tried to read
Goethe. I could never succeed . . . There is
a profligacy, an inhuman sensuality, in his
works which is utterly revolting'

Hamburg. 'The gates are shut at half-past
six o'clock . . . This idea deducts much
from the pleasure of an evening walk.' DW,
Journal, September 1798

they had come to learn German in order to make a little money by translation, but it was difficult to find anybody to speak to, and they could not afford to pay for lessons. So that they should not all talk English together, they decided to part company with Coleridge, who went to Ratzeburg, where he learned much German, while they went south to Goslar in the Harz Mountains, where they learned little. 'There is no society at Goslar,' Dorothy wrote sadly, and the severest winter of the century kept them much indoors, where they had few books. There was little to do but write, which, despite a pain in his side, a chronic complaint, William did.

The creative spirit that had produced the *Lyrical Ballads* was still upon him, but there is a difference between the Alfoxden poems, inspired mainly by the West Country, and those written at Goslar. Now homeless, his thoughts turned to his native north and early life there, and it was now that he wrote *Nutting* and began *The Prelude*, the long autobiographical poem that was meant to be an introduction to his great work 'On Man, on Nature and on Human Life', *The Recluse*. He also wrote the most haunting of his lyrics, the *Lucy* cycle. Who Lucy was is unknown; Coleridge thought she might be Dorothy, but the first line of the first poem, 'Strange fits of passion have I known', suggests that Goslar recalled memories of Orléans and Blois and his early passion for Annette. What if Annette were dead, like his love?

> *A slumber did my spirit seal;*
> *I had no human fears:*
> *She seemed a thing that could not feel*
> *The touch of earthly years.*
>
> *No motion has she now, no force;*
> *She neither hears nor sees,*
> *Rolled round in earth's diurnal course,*
> *With rocks, and stones, and trees.*

Perhaps no other poem in the language has the elemental power of these simple monosyllabic lines.

In March 1799, when the worst of winter was over, William and Dorothy made a long expedition through the Harz Mountains, and then, leaving Coleridge at Göttingen, returned to England. They made for the north, and by the beginning of May were at Sockburn, where they stayed until the end, or almost the end, of the year.

Sockburn Sockburn is a village almost surrounded by a great meander of the Tees, a few miles south of Darlington, where Tom Hutchinson had a farm, on which he was helped by his brother George, while his sisters, Mary, Sara and Joanna, kept house.

The Hutchinson house at Sockburn-on-Tees, where Wordsworth and Dorothy stayed May–December 1799. 'It is an excellent house,' Dorothy wrote, '. . . a grazing estate, and most delightfully pleasant'

Wordsworth thus renewed acquaintance with Mary Hutchinson, whom he had last seen at Racedown, and during these eight months he must have begun to think of her as his future wife. His main work during this period was the second book of *The Prelude*, which he now dedicated to Coleridge, and when Coleridge arrived at the end of October he hurried him off on a walking-tour to show him the scenes about which he was writing.

As they approached Penrith, Wordsworth learned that his younger brother John was at Newbiggin, where their Uncle Kit had suddenly died. Remembering his unhappy boyhood days with the Cooksons at Penrith, he did not call, but was rejoiced to meet John, whom he had scarcely seen since he had left school to go to sea. Coleridge, too, liked the shy young sailor 'with a swift instinct for truth and beauty', who now joined them on their tour. Cutting across the hills, they made for Hawkshead, where they found that Anne Tyson was dead, and on 3 November they left for Rydal and Grasmere. There they stayed until John returned to Penrith a few days later.

Wordsworth and Coleridge then walked north, and from Keswick William wrote to Dorothy: 'Coleridge was much struck with Grasmere and its neighbour-hood . . . There is a small house at Grasmere empty, which, perhaps, we may take;

Greta Bridge, crossed by Wordsworth and Coleridge on their way from Sockburn to Grasmere in October 1799

Dove Cottage, Grasmere, where Wordsworth lived from December 1799 to May 1808

but of this we will speak.' After an excursion to Buttermere, they returned to Penrith, where Coleridge left Wordsworth to go to London, though first he went back to Sockburn to say farewell to Dorothy and the Hutchinsons; above all, to Mary's younger sister Sara.

Wordsworth had never forgotten the hour of that 'golden summer holiday' when, as a boy, he first saw Grasmere, sighed, and murmured, 'What happy fortune were it here to live!' Apparently he went back to enquire about taking the 'small house', and on his return to Sockburn spoke to Dorothy about it, for three weeks later the two set off for Grasmere. They walked much of the way, over the hills in driving snow-showers – it was mid-winter – to Kendal, where they bought furniture, and on the evening of 21 December 1799 reached the cottage of which

they had so long dreamed, just in time to celebrate Dorothy's twenty-eighth birthday.

Dove Cottage, as it came to be called, formerly the Dove and Olive Branch Inn, stood on the right of the old coach-road from Ambleside to Keswick, facing the lake and Silver How beyond. Behind, the ground rose steeply to a little orchard, where they built a summer-house, then up to the heights of Rydal Fell, down which flowed 'the tumultuous brook of Greenhead Ghyll' to the village of Grasmere, half a mile north of the cottage at Town End. Dorothy loved the little house, up which they trained scarlet beans, her only objections being its nearness to the road, and the thinness of the partition walls, making privacy almost impossible. It was big enough for two, but not for many more, yet they were rarely without

Dove Cottage, Grasmere

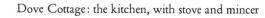

'William hurried me out in hopes that I should see her [the moon] . . .' A page from Dorothy's Grasmere *Journal*, 8 July 1802, the day before they left for France to see Annette

Dove Cottage: the kitchen, with stove and mincer

Grasmere, looking north towards Dove Cottage and Dunmail Raise, the pass to Keswick.
Helm Crag is on the left

John Wordsworth's ship, the East Indiaman, the *Earl of Abergavenny* 'the finest ship in the fleet'

John Wordsworth visitors. To their great delight, John came in January, to stay until he took up his new command as captain of the East Indiaman, the *Earl of Abergavenny*, in September. Then, in March came Mary Hutchinson, of whom John was very fond, and no sooner had Mary gone in April than Coleridge arrived. If Wordsworth would not return to the Quantocks, Coleridge must come to the Lakes. He found a house, Greta Hall, overlooking the river at Keswick, and at the end of June brought his wife and Hartley to stay before taking possession. Thus, what Alfoxden had been to Nether Stowey, Dove Cottage soon became to Greta Hall, save that the former distance had been only three miles, whereas the new was thirteen.

Dorothy's *Journal* illustrates life at Dove Cottage in this first summer of 1800, as well as her abnormal sensibility, and the distress among the peasantry, caused by the Industrial Revolution and rising prices of the long French war. The *Journal* begins on the day that William and John 'set off into Yorkshire, cold pork in their pockets', to visit the Hutchinsons.

May 14th 1800. My heart was so full that I could hardly speak to W. when I gave him a farewell kiss. I sate a long time upon a stone at the margin of the lake, and after a flood of tears my heart was easier . . . At Rydal, a woman of the village, stout and well dressed, begged a halfpenny. She had never, she said, done it before, but these hard times! . . . O that I had a letter from William!

Greta Hall, Keswick. Mrs Coleridge and Mrs Southey were sisters, and the house was shared ▶ by the two families

18th, Sunday. A little girl from Coniston came to beg. . . . I was overtaken by two Cumberland people who complimented me upon my walking. They were going to sell cloth, and odd things which they make themselves, in Hawkshead and the neighbourhood. . . . John Fisher [brother of their daily help, Molly] talked much about the alteration of the times, and observed that in a short time there would be only two ranks of people, the very rich and the very poor, 'for those who have small estates,' says he, 'are forced to sell, and all the land goes into one hand.'

June 6th. I did not leave home, in the expectation of Wm. and John, and sitting at work till after 11 o'clock I heard a foot go to the front of the house, turn round, and open the gate. It was William! After our first joy was over, we got some tea. We did not go to bed till 4 o'clock in the morning.

10th. Wm. stuck peas. After dinner he lay down.

26th. John and I walked up to the waterfall. . . . W. caught a pike weighing $4\frac{3}{4}$ lbs.

29th. Mr and Mrs Coleridge and Hartley came.

August 1st. In the morning I copied *The Brothers*.

2nd. Wm. and Coleridge went to Keswick.

6th. William came home from Keswick.

8th. Walked over the mountains. . . . Reached Coleridge's at 11 o'clock.

9th. I walked with Coleridge in the Windy Brow woods.

31st. At 11 o'clock Coleridge came, when I was walking in the still clear

Coleridge's wife, Sara

A tarn on Haystacks,
a mountain south of Buttermere

There sometimes doth a leaping fish
Send through the tarn a lonely cheer;
The crags repeat the raven's croak,
In symphony austere;
Thither the rainbow comes – the cloud –
And mists that spread the flying shroud;
And sunbeams; and the sounding blast,
That, if it could, would hurry past;
But that enormous barrier holds it fast.

moonshine in the garden. . . . We sate and chatted till half-past three. . . . Coleridge read us a part of *Christabel*.

September 1st. W. read *Joanna* and the *Firgrove* to Coleridge. They bathed.

29th. John left us. Wm. and I parted with him in sight of Ullswater. . . . Poor fellow, my heart was right sad. I could not help thinking we should see him again, because he was only going to Penrith.

But it was John's last visit to Grasmere, a visit that inspired the writing of the almost prophetic *The Brothers*, and one of the *Poems on the Naming of Places: The Firgrove*, which they called 'John's Grove', where the 'cherished visitant' had worn a short sailor's track by pacing to and fro. Another poem in this series, written soon after arrival at Dove Cottage, was in honour of 'my sweet Mary'. More ambitious was Wordsworth's attempt to satisfy Coleridge's urgent demand for a grand philosophical poem on Man and Nature, and in April he wrote the title: *The Recluse. Book First. Part First. Home at Grasmere.* After some seven hundred lines about his cottage and companions, ending with a farewell to his early ambition to be a soldier, to the hope of filling 'The heroic trumpet with the Muse's breath', he added a resolution and a rhetorical question: 'A voice shall speak, and what will be the theme?' He had already written the answer at Alfoxden:

> *Of Truth, of Grandeur, Beauty, Love, and Hope,*
> *And melancholy Fear subdued by Faith;*
> *Of blessed consolations in distress;*
> *Of moral strength and intellectual Power;*
> *Of joy in widest commonalty spread;*
> *Of the individual Mind that keeps her own*
> *Inviolate retirement.*

There were another hundred lines, which became an Introduction to *The Excursion*, but after that no more of *The Recluse*, though he claimed that *The Excursion* was intended to be its second part, inserted between two more that were to 'consist chiefly of meditations in the Author's own person'.

He had an excuse for abandoning *The Recluse*, at least temporarily, in the preparation of a new edition of *Lyrical Ballads*, the original one having been sold out; and on the day after John's departure, Dorothy, first of William's many devoted amanuenses, finished copying the last sheet of the Preface. This was a much fuller statement of his poetic faith and aims than the 'Advertisement' of the first edition. *2nd edition of 'Lyrical Ballads'*

The true poet, he maintained, is not only a man of exceptional sensitivity, but also one who thinks long and deeply, so that poetry is 'the spontaneous overflow of powerful feelings', of a secondary emotion induced by recollection and contemplation in tranquillity of the original stimulus. (We get a glimpse of this creative process in Dorothy's note: 'William kindled, and began to write the poem.') His aim was to communicate a comparable emotion to his readers; by the imaginative use of 'a *selection* of language really used by men', to make them feel the wonder and beauty, the strangeness, in the objects and incidents of ordinary life.

There remained the question of the poems to be included in the new edition. Although Coleridge read *Christabel* twice to William and Dorothy, to their 'increasing pleasure', it was decided to omit it as being too long as well as incomplete, and when the two volumes appeared, there was only one new poem by Coleridge, *Love*, inspired by memories of Sockburn and Sara Hutchinson. This went into the first volume, the contents of which, apart from the omission of Wordsworth's *Convict*, were those of the 1798 edition, though in a different order. *The Ancient Mariner* was relegated to the end, and Wordsworth merely acknowledged 'the assistance of a Friend' in supplying it and the three other poems. It is

Derwentwater from near Keswick, looking across to Derwent Fells and Causey Pike

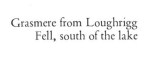

Grasmere from Loughrigg Fell, south of the lake

easy to forget how young they were; Coleridge, aged twenty-seven, deferred to the older man of thirty, whom he thought the greatest poet since Milton; but Wordsworth's treatment of his friend's work was, to say the least, inconsiderate.

All the poems in the second volume were 'By W. Wordsworth', written mostly in Goslar and the first year at Dove Cottage. The most important was the last, *Michael*, written with great difficulty towards the end of 1800: 'William worked all morning, but in vain'; 'Wm. composed without much success'; until on 9 December, 'Wm. finished his poem.' Apart from being a very moving story of a father's love for his son, it is the poem that best illustrates the practice of his poetic theory, and his philosophy of Nature leading to love of Man:

> *A story, unenriched with strange events, . . .*
> *Of Shepherds, dwellers in the valleys, men*
> *Whom I already loved; not verily*
> *For their own sakes, but for the fields and hills*
> *Where was their occupation and abode.*

On the day after the completion of *Michael*, Dorothy walked to Greta Hall – she could cover the thirteen miles in four and a half hours – where she stayed four nights; then, just before Christmas, Coleridge arrived at Dove Cottage, 'very ill, rheumatic, feverish'.

The new edition of *Lyrical Ballads* was published soon afterwards in January 1801. It attracted little attention, and Lamb, to Wordsworth's annoyance, preferred the first volume to the second. Coleridge was too ill and depressed to be greatly concerned about the reception of the poems. The damp climate of the Lakes did not suit him, and he was beginning to take opium; his marriage had broken down, and he was in love with another Sara: Sara Hutchinson, the 'Dear Asra, woman beyond utterance dear', to whom he addressed a sonnet. Worst of all perhaps, he felt that his 'shaping spirit of Imagination' was deserting him.

For the moment it had almost deserted Wordsworth. Publication always worried and exhausted him, for he would alter his work time and again before sending it to the press, even in the press, and he turned with relief to the reading of Spenser and modernization of Chaucer. He and Dorothy paid frequent visits to Greta Hall, and when Mary Hutchinson came to stay at the beginning of November, all three walked over to see Coleridge before he left for London. 'Dear, dear fellow,' wrote Dorothy. 'At last I eased my heart by weeping – nervous blubbering says William.' Sara, too, was 'in bad spirits about C'. But Mary did William good, and they spent much of their time walking together, 'cheerful, blooming and happy'. Dorothy must have known that it would not be long before they were married; then, on 21 December, a letter arrived from France: from Annette.

'Sara's Rock' beside Thirlmere, on the road between Grasmere and Keswick. On it were carved the initials· W.W. M.H. D.W. S.T.C. J.W. S.H.

Letters from Annette

A few of her letters had been smuggled across the Channel during the war, but now the situation was different. Napoleon was virtual dictator of France, but, thwarted at sea by the British navy, he wanted a breathing-space to consolidate his power and to make large-scale preparations for an invasion of England. By the end of 1801 preliminaries of peace were being arranged, and after nearly nine years of war, correspondence and travel between the two countries were again possible.

A month later Wordsworth wrote to Annette, who was living in Blois as Madame Williams, and in February he rode to Penrith to see Mary. Presumably he had already told her about Annette, but he would want to discuss the situation with her. More letters arrived from France, one from Caroline, now aged nine, and after the receipt of yet another from 'poor Annette', as Dorothy called her, 'we' resolved to go to see her. That was on 22 March, but it was to be more than three months before they started.

The year 1802 had begun badly. William was worried, unwell, and short of sleep, and many a night Dorothy, herself in miserable spirits, read her 'beloved', her 'darling', to sleep. Melancholy letters from Coleridge did not help matters. But with the return of spring and Coleridge their spirits revived, as did Wordsworth's dormant creativity. His courtship of the placid, homely Mary had done nothing to inspire him, and perhaps it was his correspondence with Annette that stirred memories of a more passionate love, and rekindled his poetry.

It is possible that he now wrote a first draft of *Vaudracour and Julia*, a story of frustrated love, not unlike that of William and Annette:

> *Her chamber-window did surpass in glory*
> *The portals of the dawn; all Paradise*
> *Could, by the simple opening of a door,*
> *Let itself in upon him.*

Nobody, ignorant of their origin, would attribute those lines to Wordsworth; they are the poetry of the young Shakespeare, of *Romeo and Juliet*. It was not that Wordsworth was still in love with Annette; his passion had been too fierce to last long, and had died in the course of nine years' separation. But he had not forgotten that passion, and we know that much of his poetry was inspired by past emotion.

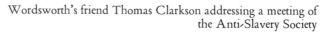

Wordsworth's friend Thomas Clarkson addressing a meeting of the Anti-Slavery Society

Dorothy gives us numerous examples of this, as well as of the speed with which he wrote poem after poem, beginning in March of this productive spring and summer of 1802. On 15 February he heard the pathetic story of a little girl who lost her cloak, and in the evening of Friday 12 March he kindled, and wrote *Alice Fell*. The next morning he wrote *The Beggar Woman*, based on Dorothy's account two years before of a woman who had called at the cottage. He finished the poem before getting up at nine on Sunday, and at breakfast, with shirt and waistcoat unbuttoned, wrote *To a Butterfly*, prompted by Dorothy's talk of their childhood, though William added that at school they used to kill white butterflies 'because they were Frenchmen'. Twelve days later he wrote *The Rainbow* while Dorothy was getting into bed, and at breakfast on the following day – 'a divine morning' – wrote 'part of an ode'. This was the *Ode on Intimations of Immortality*, in which he carried recollection back to times and regions remoter far than childhood, 'shadowy recollections . . . of that immortal sea which brought us hither'.

In April, while riding back from a visit to Mary, he composed *The Glow-worm* for Dorothy, around an incident that had occurred seven years before. Two days later, after walking with William beside Ullswater, Dorothy described in her *Journal* how the daffodils had danced and laughed under the trees beside the lake. William's recollections were often those of his sister's *Journal*, though in his poem, written two years later, he 'wandered *lonely* as a cloud'.

Ullswater, beside which the Clarksons lived. It was after visiting them that Wordsworth saw the daffodils that inspired his poem

On 3 May he began *Resolution and Independence*, the story of an old leech-gatherer whom he and Dorothy had met two years before; but on the 4th they took a holiday, and walked along the Keswick road to Wythburn. There they met Coleridge, and were drawn inevitably towards the waterfall. 'There we lay ... William and Coleridge repeated and read verses. I drank a little brandy and water, and was in heaven.' And Wordsworth continued his *Ode*:

> *The cataracts blow their trumpets from the steep; ...*
> *And all the earth is gay;*
> *Land and sea*
> *Give themselves up to jollity,*
> *And with the heart of May*
> *Doth every beast keep holiday.*

This expedition also moved him to write some Spenserian stanzas in the manner of Thomson's *Castle of Indolence*, descriptive of Coleridge and himself. Then, a few days later Dorothy read him Milton's sonnets. The form was one that he had rarely practised, as too artificial, but now he took fire, and at once wrote 'I grieved for Buonaparte', first of the hundreds of sonnets that he was to write – alas, too many! For although he wrote a score of splendid sonnets, the form, particularly the Italian, *was* too artificial for his genius: static, balanced, classical, very different from the freedom of ballad and blank verse.

Two important events occurred at this time. One was the publication of a third edition of *Lyrical Ballads*, virtually a reprint of the second, though with a revised and extended Preface. The other was the death of Lord Lonsdale, whose heir at once agreed to pay the twenty-year-old debt owed to John Wordsworth's children. This, with accrued interest, came to about £1600 each, so that William and Dorothy were now comparatively well off. 'We talked sweetly together about the disposal of our riches,' Dorothy wrote on 20 June. The first thing was to go to see Annette, and on 9 July they started.

But first, walking part of the way, they went to Tom Hutchinson's new farm near *Calais* Scarborough, Gallow Hill, where Mary was staying. Wordsworth must have discussed his forthcoming mission with her, and made arrangements for their marriage if Annette would release him. He and Dorothy then took a post-chaise to London, and early in the morning of 31 July they mounted the Dover coach and drove over Westminster Bridge: a scene that inspired the famous sonnet, 'Earth has not anything to show more fair'. Next morning they were in Calais, where they had arranged to meet Annette, and where they stayed a month. The only record of their adventure is in Dorothy's *Journal*. They lodged in a dirty and smelly neighbourhood. It was very hot, and William bathed, but she had a cold. Almost every evening they walked by the sea-shore, either with Annette

◄ 'A most beautiful sight as we crossed Westminster Bridge.' DW. 31 July 1802

'We arrived at Calais at four o'clock on Sunday morning, the 31st of July.' (1st of August?) DW

and Caroline, or alone; and there was one unforgettable night when she and William walked upon the pier. And that is all; she tells us nothing about Annette, or of what passed between her and William during that long hot month. From her letters, two of which have been discovered, Annette appears to have been an affectionate, sentimental woman, and perhaps it took these four weeks to persuade her to agree to separation. There was also the question of Caroline's future to be discussed. Wordsworth wrote a sonnet to her, and on 29 August he and Dorothy sailed for Dover.

He was depressed by the France he saw, so different from the France first seen with Robert Jones in the delirious days of the early Revolution; he detested Napoleon and the servility of the people towards him; he loathed the tyranny that drove Negroes out of the country, and he said so in a series of sonnets. It was good to be back in England, to see and hear English sights and sounds, and again he said so in a sonnet: 'Europe is yet in bonds; . . . but thou art free, My Country!' Yet he was not happy about what he saw in London. England had need of another Milton: 'She is a fen of stagnant waters . . . We are selfish men.'

They stayed three weeks in London, where they saw their brothers: Richard, the London solicitor, John, just back from his first East India voyage, and Christopher, a Fellow of Trinity, Cambridge. On 24 September they were back at Gallow Hill.

Marries Mary Hutchinson

Ten days later, William and Mary Hutchinson were married in Brompton church. Dorothy was too overcome to attend the ceremony, threw herself on her bed, and lay still, until she heard that the couple were approaching, when she ran out of the house and fell upon the bosom of her beloved William. After breakfast they – William, Mary and Dorothy – left for Grasmere in a chaise. They were a strange trio: the proud, dedicated poet, who had just abandoned his first love; his plain, reticent wife; and his little, neurotic, gipsy-faced sister. They stopped at Kirby, where they sauntered in the churchyard and read the gravestones. Then at Wensley they joined the road along which Dorothy had walked so joyfully with her brother three years before, as she first approached 'the home in which we were to rest'. Here her *Journal* makes almost tragic reading: 'My heart melted away with dear recollections – the bridge, the little waterspout, the steep hill, the church. They are among the most vivid of my inner visions.' And Staveley was 'the first mountain village I came to with William, when we first began our pilgrimage together'. They reached Dove Cottage 'at about 6 o'clock on Wednesday evening, the 6th of October, 1802'. William had got a second helpmate and devoted amanuensis. Too devoted, perhaps; for a year later Coleridge was to write a revealing letter to his Stowey friend Thomas Poole: 'I saw him more and more benetted in hypochondriacal Fancies, living wholly among *Devotees* – having every the minutest Thing, almost his very eating and drinking, done for

Brompton Church. 'On Monday, 4th October 1802, my brother William was married to Mary Hutchinson.' DW

him by his Sister, or Wife – and I trembled, lest a Film should rise, and thicken his moral Eye.'

The first of Mary's five children, John, was born in June 1803, and two months later William and Dorothy left her, to go to Scotland with Coleridge 'in search of scenery'. They visited the grave of Burns at Dumfries, but after a fortnight of rain in the Highlands 'poor Coleridge, being very unwell', decided to return home. This is Dorothy's account; but Coleridge wanted to escape from Wordsworth, whom he found 'hypochondriacal . . . silent and self-centred', and instead

Children

Scotland

'Went to the churchyard where Burns is buried . . . There is no stone to mark the spot; but a hundred guineas have been collected, to be expended on some sort of monument.' DW. 18 August 1803

(*Right*) Melrose Abbey. 'In the street met Mr Scott, who gave us a cordial greeting, and conducted us thither himself.' DW. 19 September 1803

of making for home he walked vigorously north before returning to Greta Hall, where his family had been joined by that of his brother-in-law Southey. A month later William and Dorothy ended their tour with a visit to Walter Scott, who showed them the ruins of Melrose Abbey, and read them part of *The Lay of the Last Minstrel*. By the end of September they were back at Dove Cottage, where they found Mary very well, and little John asleep in the clothes-basket by the fire. A number of fine poems were inspired by this Scottish tour: among them, *Stepping Westward*, *The Solitary Reaper*, and *Yarrow Unvisited*.

At Dumbarton Castle, the cannon, regular soldiers, and yeomanry cavalry had reminded them of the fears of invasion. For by this time the war against France, or rather against Napoleon, now First Consul and about to become Emperor, had been renewed. His first object was the invasion of England, for which he had assembled a formidable army at Boulogne, and Wordsworth replied with a series of patriotic sonnets, and by enlisting in the Grasmere Volunteers. 'Surely there never was a more determined hater of the French,' wrote Dorothy. It was just ten years since he had rejoiced when Englishmen were defeated by the French; but then there had been no Napoleon, now the personification of tyranny. Coleridge did not join the Volunteers; he was a sick man. The Wordsworths were prepared to move with him to a more congenial climate, but in January 1804, well stocked with laudanum, he left Grasmere in search of better health in Malta. It was to be nearly three years before they saw him again.

Coleridge goes abroad

'We are to go to Ambleside on Sunday to be mustered, and put on, for the first time, our military apparel.' George III reviewing volunteers. 4 June 1799

The invasion scare, 1803–5. Attack by air, sea and underground. A French fantasy

Napoleon crowns himself
Emperor, 2 December 1804

East Indiamen, including John Wordsworth's *Earl of Abergavenny*, attack a French fleet in the Straits of Malacca, 15 February 1804

Wordsworth now settled down to complete *The Prelude*, the long autobiographical poem describing the growth of a poet's mind, though 'settled down' gives a false impression, for most of his poetry was composed while walking, and then dictated to one of his willing scribes. To sit with a pen in his hand brought on a pain in his chest, a perspiration, and reduced him to a bundle of uneasiness. There was an interruption in August when his daughter Dorothy, or Dora, was born, a girl destined to become the fourth of his willing helpers; there were already three, for Mary's entertaining sister Sara had just come to live with them.

Death of John

Then, in February 1805, came the shattering news that John had been drowned when his ship was wrecked off Portland Bill. Dorothy was prostrated, and Wordsworth expressed his grief in a number of poems, characteristically finding comfort in the flowers that John had loved, the daisy, and the moss campion that grew near Grisedale Tarn, where they had parted from him after his long stay at Dove Cottage four years before. John had hoped to make money to help his brother, and to retire to Grasmere, perhaps as Sara's husband.

An event that vividly recalled his death occurred in October: the Battle of Trafalgar, in which Nelson was mortally wounded. Wordsworth was not a great admirer of Nelson as a man, and his *Character of the Happy Warrior*, 'the generous Spirit . . . a Soul whose master-bias leans / To homefelt pleasures and to gentler scenes', was a tribute to his brother rather than to the admiral.

Trafalgar put an end to Napoleon's plans for invading England, and he now loosed his armies on Britain's allies. In December he shattered the Austrians at Austerlitz, in 1806 routed the Prussians at Jena ('Another year! another deadly blow!') and in 1807 defeated the Russians at Friedland. Once again Britain stood alone, and she had lost the minister who had guided her through the long perilous years of war: Pitt, killed, it was said, by the news of Austerlitz.

(*Below left*) Weymouth Bay and Portland Bill. 'I think of Wordsworth, for on that spot [6 February 1805] perished his brother in the wreck of the *Abergavenny*.' John Constable

(*Right*) 'The lamentable news which your letter brought . . .' Wordsworth writes to his elder brother Richard, 11 February 1805

'Few men have ever died under circumstances so likely to make their death of benefit to their country.' The death of Nelson after Trafalgar, 21 October 1805

My dear Brother,

The lamentable news which your letter brought has now been known to us seven hours during which time I have done all in my power to alleviate the distress of poor Dorothy and my wife. — Mary & I were walking out when the letter came: it was brought by Sarah Hutchinson who had come from Kendale where she was staying; to be of use in the house & to comfort us: so that I had no power of breaking the force of the shock to Dorothy or to Mary. They are both very ill, Dorothy especially on whom this loss of her beloved Brother will I fear take deep hold. I shall do my best to console her; but John was very dear to all & my heart will never forget him. God rest his soul!

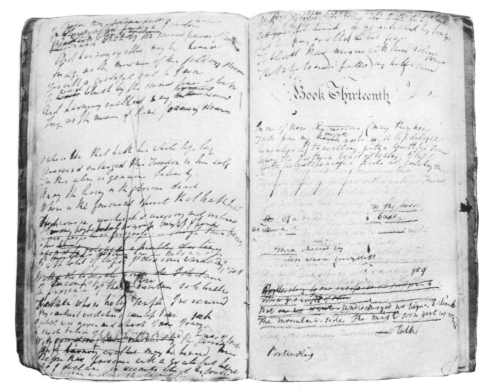

'In one of those excursions . . .' Opening lines of the last Book of *The Prelude*, describing the ascent of Snowdon. The writing is Sara Hutchinson's

Piel Castle in a Storm, by Sir George Beaumont

Sir George Beaumont (1753–1827). 'A painter's eye, a poet's heart'

(*Above right*) Wordsworth in 1806, aged 36. 'His eyes are not, under any circumstances, bright, lustrous, or piercing; but after a day's toil in walking, I have seen them assume an appearance the most solemn and spiritual that it is possible for the human eye to wear.' De Quincey

Wordsworth finished *The Prelude* in 1805 – though it was to be much revised in later years – and in the spring of 1806 he went to London, where he stayed part of the time with Sir George Beaumont, a wealthy patron of the arts, to whom Coleridge had introduced him in 1803. Beaumont was such an admirer of the *Lyrical Ballads* that he presented Wordsworth with a piece of land near Keswick, so that he could build a house there, and live near Coleridge. The house was never built, but Beaumont now commissioned the miniaturist Henry Edridge to make a drawing of him. Beaumont was himself an enthusiastic, though undistinguished painter, and it was on this visit that Wordsworth saw his picture of *Piel Castle in a Storm*, which again reminded him of John's death, and suggested the *Elegiac Stanzas* in which he mourned the loss of the visionary power, of 'The light that never was, on sea or land', which had suffused the castle when he stayed near it twelve years before. But now, 'A deep distress hath humanised my Soul'.

Sir George Beaumont

His two months' absence from the confined domesticity of his little cottage, from three devoted women and two young children, did him good, but in June, soon after his return, he greeted another arrival, a third child, Thomas. Having finished *The Prelude*, he resumed work on *The Recluse*, or rather, developed *The Ruined Cottage*, which became the first book of *The Excursion*. It was written to please Coleridge; and at last came the long-hoped-for news of his return to London.

Coleridge returns

The Wordsworths were preparing to spend the winter in a farmhouse on Sir George Beaumont's estate at Coleorton in Leicestershire, and there Coleridge joined them. They were shocked by his appearance; opium and brandy had ruined his health; no longer gamesome as a boy, his limbs tossing in delight, he was a puffy, dejected, middle-aged man, reluctant to recall their former happy days together. Wordsworth tried to renew their old relations by reading him the last books of *The Prelude*, written during his absence in Malta, but the conclusion was almost unbearable for the 'beloved friend' to whom it was dedicated:

> *That summer, under whose indulgent skies,*
> *Upon smooth Quantock's airy ridge we roved*
> *Unchecked, or loitered 'mid the sylvan combes,*
> *Thou in bewitching words, with happy heart,*
> *Didst chaunt the vision of that Ancient Man,*
> *The bright-eyed Mariner . . .*
> *And a comfort now hath risen*
> *From hope that thou art near, and wilt be soon*
> *Restored to us in renovated health . . .*
> *What we have loved,*
> *Others will love, and we will teach them how.*

It was not to be, and Coleridge, moved to tears by that circle of beloved faces, implored his friend not to injure the memory of his communion with his nobler mind by pity or grief.

Coleridge's poem sent to Sir George Beaumont in January 1807

Coleorton, near Ashby-de-la-Zouche, built 1802–10 for Sir George Beaumont by George Dance, who also drew his portrait (p. 81)

To W. Wordsworth

Lines composed, for the greater part on the Night in which I
finished the recitation of his Poem (in thirteen Books) concerning the growth
and history of his own mind. Jan.ʸ 7, 1807. Cole-orton, near Ashby de la Zouch

O Friend! O Teacher! God's great Gift to me!
Into my heart have I receiv'd that Lay
More than historic, that prophetic Lay,
Wherein (high theme by Thee first sung aright)
Of the Foundations and the Building-up
Of thy own Spirit, thou hast lov'd to tell
What may be told; to the' understanding mind

There must have been an unhealthy, febrile atmosphere in the Coleorton house that winter: Dorothy in love with Coleridge, Coleridge in love with Sara, torturing himself with the suspicion that she was in love with William, and William depressed by the change that had made him poor. Yet, in spite of his depression, he was able to write the *Song at the Feast of Brougham Castle*, and describe what they had loved, like the good Lord Clifford:

> *Love had he found in huts where poor men lie;*
> *His daily teachers had been woods and rills,*
> *The silence that is in the starry sky,*
> *The sleep that is among the lonely hills.*

'Poems in Two Volumes'
The *Song* was among the *Poems in Two Volumes* published in 1807, containing most of his work, apart from *The Prelude*, written since the second edition of the *Lyrical Ballads*. Although now recognized as containing many of his finest poems, *Resolution and Independence*, *Stepping Westward* and *The Solitary Reaper*, for example,

'I, dear Sara – *I* am blessing *thee*.'
Coleridge's letter to Asra

'Asra': Sara Hutchinson

'Such change;'
Coleridge *c.* 1807

the volumes were fodder for the wit of contemporary reviewers. The matter was low, trivial, silly: daisies, butterflies, redbreasts, little girls and leech-gatherers, and the manner, apart from the sonnets, equally puerile. Wordsworth was, or affected to be, undisturbed, and proudly wrote to Lady Beaumont: 'My ears are stone-dead to this idle buzz, and my flesh as insensible as iron to these petty stings.' But it was not true; they were spiritually deadly. Well aware of his genius, immensely proud, and lacking a sense of humour, the ability to laugh at himself, he found ridicule even worse than neglect, and behind that north-country mask of reserve, resentment began to constrict his generous impulses, to infect the pure source of his inspiration.

White she is as lily of June,
And beauteous as the silver moon.

(The White Doe of Rylstone).

Gordale-chasm, terrific as the lair
Where the young lions couch.

Thomas de Quincey (1785–1859). 'Very diminutive in person . . . and so modest, and so very shy.' DW

Coleridge left Coleorton for the West Country in April, and at midsummer the Wordsworths returned to Grasmere. On the way they visited the Yorkshire dales and Bolton Abbey, a scene that inspired the mystical *White Doe of Rylstone*, written in the winter of 1807.

It was now that Wordsworth first met Thomas de Quincey, a shy young man, who called on his way to Keswick. The Wordsworths liked him so much that when they left Dove Cottage they sublet it to him, and there he lived for many years. He later wrote a description of Wordsworth as he first saw him: his face long, with a broad forehead; eyes rather small, but sometimes assuming the most solemn and spiritual appearance; the nose a little arched, and large, 'accounted an unequivocal expression of animal appetites'; the mouth and its 'circum-jacencies' the strongest feature in the face, which reminded him of a portrait of Milton.

As another baby was expected in 1808, and Coleridge, estranged from his wife, *Allan Bank* was likely to be a semi-permanent member of the family, in May the Wordsworths left Dove Cottage for a bigger house. This was Allan Bank, to the west of Gras-mere church, a house that was visually repulsive to Wordsworth, and almost uninhabitable in winter owing to smoky chimneys, but at least large enough to accommodate William, Mary, Dorothy, Sara, and the three children, as well as the new baby Catherine and Coleridge, who arrived together, in September. In addition, there were Coleridge's two sons, Hartley and Derwent, who sometimes came over from their school in Ambleside.

Coleridge was in better spirits, and preparing to produce a weekly literary and political paper, *The Friend*. Wordsworth also turned to politics and prose, for a new international situation had arisen. The Peninsular War had begun.

Napoleon had occupied Spain, forced its king to abdicate, and placed his own brother Joseph on the throne. The Spanish people rose against the invaders, and a small British army under Arthur Wellesley, later Duke of Wellington, landed in Portugal to support them. Wellesley defeated the French at Vimiero, but his superior officers agreed to the Convention of Cintra, whereby the French army was allowed to withdraw intact with all its equipment. 'Never did any public event cause in my mind so much sorrow', wrote Wordsworth, and he voiced his indignation and that of England in a pamphlet, *The Convention of Cintra*. He was always a passionate defender of liberty, both individual and national – he had already written sonnets on *The Extinction of the Venetian Republic* and *The Subjugation of Switzerland* – and now he wrote this eloquent plea for the right of all nations, not only Spain, to liberty and self-determination. It was too rhetorical, however, and its publication was so long delayed that it had little effect.

Sir Arthur Wellesley's quarters at Vimiero, August 1808

(*Above*) *The Third of May, 1808*,
Goya. Execution of Spanish
volunteers by the French

'O sorrow and shame for
our country!'

CONCERNING

THE RELATIONS

OF

GREAT BRITAIN,
SPAIN, AND PORTUGAL,

TO EACH OTHER, AND TO THE COMMON ENEMY,

AT THIS CRISIS;

AND SPECIFICALLY AS AFFECTED BY

THE

CONVENTION OF CINTRA:

The whole brought to the test of those Principles, by which
alone the Independence and Freedom of Nations
can be Preserved or Recovered.

Qui didicit patriæ quid debet ;————
Quod sit conscripti, quod judicis officium ; quæ
Partes in bellum missi ducis.

BY WILLIAM WORDSWORTH.

London:

PRINTED FOR LONGMAN, HURST, REES, AND ORME,
PATERNOSTER-ROW.

1809.

Wordsworth rarely wrote essays and articles to raise money, which does not mean that he was uninterested in money; he published the *Lyrical Ballads* 'for money and money alone', and always extracted the best price he could from his publishers. But in spite of his frugal way of living, expenses, like prices, were constantly mounting in the bigger house, and he followed the *Cintra* pamphlet with an essay describing the scenery of the English Lakes. This was an introduction to a volume of drawings by the Rev. Joseph Wilkinson, published in 1810 as *Select Views in Cumberland, Westmorland and Lancashire*. Wordsworth's name did not appear, probably because he was ashamed of the prints, which he thought 'intolerable', but it was added when his essay was published separately in 1822, after which it became a popular *Guide to the Lakes*.

After months of delay, the first number of Coleridge's *The Friend* appeared in June 1809, but it was December before Wordsworth made his first contribution. This was a reply to a correspondent calling himself 'Mathetes': really John Wilson, a wealthy young man with a house on Windermere, later to become famous as 'Christopher North' of *Blackwood's Magazine*. Wilson had asked for advice to the young on entering the adult world, hoping to get a reply from Wordsworth, whom he greatly admired; and in his *Letter to Mathetes* Wordsworth advised a young man to learn to understand himself, and then return to contemplation of 'the Visible Universe, and to conversation with Ancient Books'. He had already given the same advice to young de Quincey: 'Love Nature and Books, and you will be happy.' Yet he himself was never a great reader, and later admitted that he was not spending a shilling a year on new books, including periodicals. His only other contribution to *The Friend* was an *Essay on Epitaphs*, in which he confessed that he would find no happiness in life if he were not convinced of the immortality of some part of his being.

The essay served almost as an epitaph on *The Friend*, which had miraculously survived for more than six months, but expired early in 1810. That it had not been stillborn was owing to the devotion of Sara Hutchinson, who acted as Coleridge's secretary, and tried, though unsuccessfully, to wean him from drugs and brandy. He was still miserably in love with 'Asra', and when, no longer able to stand the strain, she left Allan Bank for a long visit to her brother Tom, he shut himself in his room, rarely spoke, and wrote nothing.

Quarrel with Coleridge Shortly before Mary's fifth child William was born in May, Coleridge went to Keswick, but when Basil Montagu and his wife came to stay at Allan Bank, they proposed taking him to live with them in London, in the hope of curing him. Wordsworth naturally had to tell Montagu about Coleridge's habits, and among other things said something about his having been 'for years an absolute nuisance in the family'. Unfortunately Montagu told Coleridge what Wordsworth had said: according to Coleridge, not only that he had been 'an absolute nuisance',

Henry Crabb Robinson (1775–1867). In 1808 he went to Spain as special war correspondent for *The Times*. It was in this year that Lamb introduced him to Wordsworth, whose manners he found 'not prepossessing', though he felt 'an high respect for him'

but also that Wordsworth had no hope of 'a rotten drunkard' who had 'rotted his entrails out by intemperance' – apparently his confusion of a flippant remark made by Wordsworth on parting. Montagu wrote to tell him that he had repeated his warnings, but Wordsworth failed to write to explain or apologize to Coleridge, who was heartbroken at what he considered a betrayal of fifteen years' friendship and 'almost superstitious idolatry'. It was eighteen months before they were reconciled, mainly by the efforts of Henry Crabb Robinson, a journalist turned barrister, one of the most attractive men of the age, whom Wordsworth had recently met, and who was to become one of his closest friends. Yet the reconciliation was incomplete; Coleridge never again visited the Wordsworths, and to his Stowey friend Thomas Poole he wrote: 'All thoughts and admiration will be the same – *are* the same, but – aye, there remains an immedicable *But*.'

It is difficult to decide how far, if at all, Wordsworth was to blame for the estrangement, but it is worth noting that Lamb's sympathies were with Coleridge, and that he thought Wordsworth 'cold'. And even Robinson, in whose opinion Wordsworth had behaved with the most scrupulous delicacy, was shocked when, five years after the quarrel, he witnessed the first meeting of the two at a party in London: 'The manner of Coleridge towards Wordsworth was most respectful, but Wordsworth towards Coleridge was cold and scornful.'

It was ironical that just before the beginning of the misunderstanding Words-worth had resumed work on *The Excursion*, which he intended to be part of *The Recluse*, the poem that Coleridge had always wanted him to write, but in which he no longer showed any interest. It was finished soon after the reconcili-ation, but not at Allan Bank, for in June 1811 the Wordsworths moved into a smaller and less extravagant house.

This was Grasmere Parsonage, close to the church, where they had 'at least one sitting-room clear of smoke in all winds'. Shelley was in the Lakes that winter, and met Southey, but failed to meet Wordsworth, though he wrote: 'Wordsworth (a *quondam* associate of Southey) yet retains the integrity of his independence, but his poverty is such that he is frequently obliged to beg for a shirt to his back.' Wordsworth was never an associate of Southey, who shared Greta Hall with his sister-in-law Mrs Coleridge, but as she was jealous of Dorothy, there was little contact between the two houses, and the poets, though friendly, rarely met. And Shelley's remark about Wordsworth's shirt was playful exaggeration; Wordsworth was poor, but not poverty-stricken, and he was soon unhappily to be relieved of two of his charges.

Death of two Children   While he was in London in June 1812, his three-year-old daughter Catherine died, and in December the six-year-old Thomas, 'of all the children, the one who . . . gave us the purest delight,' wrote Dorothy. And she added: 'At times I think my brother looks ten years older since the death of Thomas.' If we remember Wordsworth's love, adoration almost, of children, the change is understandable;

'The Parsonage of Grasmere', where Wordsworth lived from June 1811 to May 1813. Two of his children died here

The Stamp Office, Ambleside. Wordsworth was Distributor from 1813 to 1842

and it was now that he began to have trouble with his eyes, and a fear that he might go blind.

His integrity of independence was not to last much longer. He had already asked Lord Lonsdale if he could help him to a position that would augment his income without taking up too much of his time, and in March 1813 Lonsdale was able to offer him the office of Distributor of Stamps for Westmorland. It was a responsible post, involving the stamping of legal documents, but, helped by a clerk, not very onerous, and was worth about £300 a year, a sum that increased with the years and extension of the area of his Distributorship.

Stamp Distribution

He was now in a position to change houses again. The old Parsonage, over-looking the churchyard where the two children were buried, had become intolerable to the whole family, and in May 1813 they left Grasmere for Rydal Mount, high on a spur of the hills, looking south towards Ambleside and Windermere, and west towards Rydal; a roomy and comfortable house that was to be Wordsworth's home for the rest of his life. A few months after the move, Southey was appointed the new Poet Laureate.

Rydal Mount

Southey as Poet Laureate. The quotation is from his *Wat Tyler*, a poem of his republican youth

A POET MOUNTED on the COURT-PEGASUS.

Aye, aye, hear him—
He is no mealy mouthed court orator
To flatter vice, and pamper lordly pride!!
vide Wat Tyler.

93

Interior of summer house,
at Rydal Mount

The Upper Fall, Rydal.

With sparkling foam, a small cascade
Illumines from within the leafy shade.

Rydal Mount, where Wordsworth lived from 1813 till his death in 1850. 'It is a modest mansion of a sober hue, with two tiers of five windows.' CW

As Mary was slow to recover from the shock of the loss of her two children, in the following summer Wordsworth took her and Sara for a holiday in Scotland. Travelling in the jaunting-car that Dorothy, Coleridge, and he had used eleven years before, they reached Inverness before turning south for Edinburgh and Scott's new house at Abbotsford, near Melrose. On the way they called on the poet James Hogg, the 'Ettrick Shepherd', who took them to see the River Yarrow, unvisited by William and Dorothy in 1803: an expedition that led to the writing of *Yarrow Visited*.

'The Excursion'   By this time *The Excursion* had been published, a poem of some 9,000 lines, comparable in length to *Paradise Lost*, and it should be remembered what store Wordsworth set by this work of many years and epic proportions. In April he had written to Poole: 'I have at last resolved to send to the press a portion of a poem which, if I live to finish it, I hope future times will "not willingly let die". These

Abbotsford, the house that Walter Scott built on land on the south of the Tweed, bought in 1811

Scott, created a baronet in 1820, with friends at Abbotsford. An imaginary scene

you know are the words of my great predecessor . . .' He thought of himself as the successor of Milton, but this was not the comparison that occurred to most of his readers and reviewers. It is true that Lamb admired the poem, 'the noblest conversational poem I ever read'; so did Hazlitt, though he disliked the 'intellectual egotism' of the author, the ventriloquist who spoke through the mouths of all his characters. Even Crabb Robinson had to admit that there were 'passages which run heavily, tales which are prolix', and feared that Wordsworth might be charged with 'dulness'. Coleridge was frankly disappointed, and told Wordsworth so; *The Excursion* was inferior to *The Prelude*. He was reluctant to suggest any flagging of the writer's genius, and wondered if the inferiority 'might have been occasioned by the influence of self-established convictions having given to certain thoughts and expressions a depth and force which they have not for readers in general'. A polite way of saying that his opinions were platitudes.

James Hogg
(1770–1835)

Francis Jeffrey in the *Edinburgh Review* agreed, though in language less polite: 'a tissue of moral and devotional ravings, in which innumerable changes are rung upon a few very simple and familiar ideas . . . a hubbub of strange raptures and fantastical sublimities . . . interminable dulness of mellifluous extravagance . . . mystical verbiage of the Methodist pulpit'.

There was truth as well as ill-mannered hyperbole in Jeffrey's strictures. After the profound simplicity and freshness, the elemental inevitability, of the earlier poems, *The Excursion* is certainly disappointing. There are fine and moving passages, but many of these are earlier work: the story of Margaret in Book I, for example, was originally written in 1797, and Book IV, with its description of ancient Greece, in 1806:

> *A beardless youth, who touched a golden lute,*
> *And filled the illumined groves with ravishment . . .*

No wonder Keats loved these lines: he might have written them himself. But the Wordsworth who wrote the Preface to the *Lyrical Ballads* would not have called the sun 'the shining giver of the day', or a mother 'The thankful captive of maternal bonds'. Nor would he have written like this, the kind of passage that prompted Byron's gibe, 'a drowsy, frowsy poem':

> *And further; by contemplating these Forms*
> *In the relations which they bear to man,*
> *We shall discern how, through the various means*
> *Which silently they yield, are multiplied*
> *The spiritual presences of absent things.*

He was forgetting that poetry is not so much the thing said as the way of saying it; that it is made with words, not with opinions. It used to be 'Let Nature be your

◀ The Solitary's Cottage, Blea Tarn:

A liquid pool that glittered in the sun,
And one bare dwelling; one abode, no more!

(*The Excursion*, II.338–9)

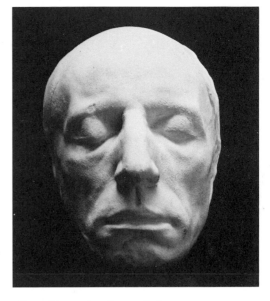

'I had a cast made yesterday [12 May 1815] of
Wordsworth's face. He bore it like a philosopher.'
B.R. Haydon

teacher'. Now it was 'Let Wordsworth'. All too often, 'Let Wordsworth be your preacher'.

It was not that he was finished as a poet, but the fire was dying, the flash of inspired perception becoming rarer; and it is not too much to say that the work that places him among the very greatest of English poets, indeed of all poets, was written in the decade 1798–1808, the period of Alfoxden, Goslar and Dove Cottage. Matthew Arnold recognized this when he wrote the Preface to his selection of Wordsworth's poems in 1879, and since then most critics have agreed with him, though they have differed as to the cause of the decline. H.W. Garrod attributed it to the loss of Coleridge's companionship; Herbert Read to the delayed action of remorse for his desertion of Annette.

More probably the poet deteriorated because the man changed so at about the age of forty. It is fashionable to maintain that there were not two Wordsworths: the young, inspired radical, and the old, prosy conservative. But this is to do injustice to the first Wordsworth, the great poet. The young man was not father of the old, his days were not bound each to each by natural piety, as he had hoped. It is true that he always remained a humanitarian, the champion of liberty and the oppressed; in *The Excursion* he attacked the abuse of child labour in factories, and advocated a system of national education – under the direction of the Established Church. It is also true that before he was forty he had modified the revolutionary opinions of the youth of twenty-two. But half-way through his life there came a change that was something more than a transition from generous youth to cautious middle-age.

There were a number of possible reasons for this, and their effect would be cumulative. Coleridge had mentioned one as early as 1803, when he trembled lest the ministrations of two devoted women, since increased to three, should corrupt his moral eye. He was over-domesticated, too comfortable. By 1807 Coleridge was a wreck, and Wordsworth had lost the man who had been an inspiration for the last ten years. By 1812 he had lost the friend. In the same year he lost two of his children. But the main cause of the change was probably the corroding, concealed resentment at the neglect and ridicule of his poetry, and when in 1813 his neighbour Southey, of whom he thought highly as a *prose* writer, was made Poet Laureate, he may have felt more than a twinge of envy; and envy, he knew, 'was very dangerous for *me*'. So were quarrels, grief, and resentment: all spiritually exhausting, destructive of integrity, of delicate perception, and imagination. Pride became a defensive arrogance, self-confidence became egotism, reserve loquacity, originality conventionality, courage timidity, independence deference. He sought advancement in other ways, courted the patronage of Lord Lonsdale, accepted money from him and a lucrative post. This involved a change of allegiance, and by the time he moved into Rydal Mount the radical pantheist had become an Anglican Tory, opposed to any change in the established order, frightened of the unrest among the 'lower classes'.

He said he would shed his blood for the Church Establishment, and considered the combination of workers very alarming. 'W. anticipates a renewal of all the horrors of war between the poor and the rich; a conflict of property with no property,' Crabb Robinson wrote in 1812. Property! From Sir George Beaumont he had accepted the small estate of Applethwaite near Keswick, he had allowed Lord Lonsdale to help him to buy another near Ullswater, and he had invested in two more. Only property owners had the right to vote. His conception of liberty did not include the liberty of the workers to vote, or to form trade unions to better their conditions. A paternal State and maternal Church best knew what was good for them.

Lowther Castle, near Penrith, built for Lord Lonsdale by Robert Smirke, 1808–10

Wordsworth in 1817. 'William was *delighted* with the beauty of his picture.' SH

Of course a Tory churchman may also be a great poet, but the point is that he could not have written Wordsworth's early poetry, and the transformed Words-worth was rarely able to write anything comparable to this. His new allegiances were at odds with his native genius. He protested that he was the happiest of men, but the joy had gone out of his poetry; he had written the poet's epitaph:

> *But who is He, with modest looks,*
> *And clad in homely russet brown?*
> *He murmurs near the running brooks*
> *A music sweeter than their own . . .*
>
> *The outward shows of sky and earth,*
> *Of hill and valley, he has viewed;*
> *And impulses of deeper birth*
> *Have come to him in solitude.*

In *Laodamia*, written in 1814, he abandoned his old friends, the peasants and wanderers of Grasmere, and returned to the classical subjects of the eighteenth century, advising his heroine

> *to control*
> *Rebellious passion: for the Gods approve*
> *The depth, and not the tumult, of the soul.*

It was the rebellious passion and tumultuous soul of the former Wordsworth that had inspired the *Lucy* poems and lyrics, and now he was preaching control.

Laodamia loved her husband too passionately, and died, but she was allowed 'to gather flowers . . . 'mid unfading bowers'. Not for long, however; a few years later Wordsworth doomed her 'to wander / Apart from happy ghosts that gather flowers'. He had become stiff, inflexible, cold.

The Excursion was dedicated to the 'illustrious Peer' Lord Lonsdale, and the first collected edition of his *Poems* in 1815 to Sir George Beaumont. He was entering more exalted circles, and his move to Rydal Mount brought him and his family into the genteel society of Ambleside and Windermere, very different from the secluded rusticity of Grasmere and his former humble neighbours. It was now that he quarrelled with de Quincey, his tenant at Dove Cottage. De Quincey had fallen in love with a farmer's daughter, who bore him a child before he married her in 1816. The ladies of Rydal Mount were indignant at this liaison with a 'low-born woman'; so was Wordsworth, who refused to visit him, and their friendship was at an end. Yet de Quincey married his Margaret, and Wordsworth had not married Annette. He did not even join Annette in Paris when their daughter Caroline married Jean-Baptiste Baudouin in 1816, though he made Caroline an allowance of £30 a year. He was busy writing, and *End of French* preparing for hasty publication, odes and sonnets in celebration of Waterloo and *War* Napoleon's downfall.

Their rhetoric and false sentiment make embarrassing reading: 'The tubed engine', the organ, that is, peals in praise of the 'Intrepid sons of Albion' who 'quelled that impious crew', loving death better than life, when duty and the God of Battles called them to 'bleed in open war'.

The Tory The post-war years 1815–22 in Britain were a period of great distress, violent unrest, and repression by the Tory Government. Starving workers marched on London, and as Habeas Corpus was suspended, some were imprisoned without

Peterloo, 16 August 1819

trial. In 1819, when a political meeting in St Peter's Fields, Manchester, was charged by the yeomanry, eight people were killed and four hundred injured. The Government followed up this success with the Six Acts, which forbade such meetings, and imposed a fourpenny stamp duty on newspapers, measures that led to an attempt to murder the whole Cabinet. In 1814 Wordsworth had written to Lord Lonsdale: 'If the whole island was covered with a force of this kind [an armed yeomanry], the Press properly curbed, the Poor Laws gradually reformed, provision made for new Churches . . . order may yet be preserved among us, and the people remain free and happy.' The 'Manchester Massacre', or 'Peterloo', as it was derisively called, was necessary for the preservation of order.

In 1818 Hazlitt delivered a course of *Lectures on the Living Poets,* in which he paid tribute to Wordsworth as the most original of all, the author of poems 'of inconceivable beauty'. He was thinking of the *Lyrical Ballads* and *Poems* of 1807; but *The Excursion* was a failure, and he finished with an attack on 'the Lake school of poetry': Wordsworth, Coleridge and Southey. A few years later, in *The Spirit of the Age,* he wrote one of the most penetrating of all appreciations of Wordsworth, mingling generous praise with a few stinging asides: 'If he is become verbose and oracular of late years, he was not so in his better days.' 'But', he added, 'the sense of injustice and of undeserved ridicule sours the temper and narrows the views.' It was true; if Wordsworth's genius had been recognized by the time

◀ Waterloo, 18 June 1815

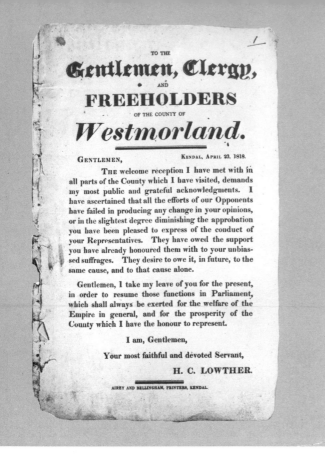

TO THE
Gentlemen, Clergy,
AND
FREEHOLDERS
OF THE COUNTY OF
Westmorland.

GENTLEMEN,   KENDAL, APRIL 23, 1818.

THE welcome reception I have met with in all parts of the County which I have visited, demands my most public and grateful acknowledgments. I have ascertained that all the efforts of our Opponents have failed in producing any change in your opinions, or in the slightest degree diminishing the approbation you have been pleased to express of the conduct of your Representatives. They have owed the support you have already honoured them with to your unbiassed suffrages. They desire to owe it, in future, to the same cause, and to that cause alone.

Gentlemen, I take my leave of you for the present, in order to resume those functions in Parliament, which shall always be exerted for the welfare of the Empire in general, and for the prosperity of the County which I have the honour to represent.

I am, Gentlemen,

Your most faithful and devoted Servant,

H. C. LOWTHER.

AIREY AND BELLINGHAM, PRINTERS, KENDAL.

Henry Brougham, the Whig,
who opposed the Lowthers

The Westmorland Election, 1818. Colonel
H. C. Lowther was the younger son of the Earl
of Lonsdale

he was forty-five, he would have been able to love new things, which he confessed he was by then unable to do.

Wordsworth did not like Hazlitt, whom he had come to suspect of immoral behaviour in a Keswick escapade many years before, and Hazlitt knew that Wordsworth 'would not forgive a single censure, mingled with however great a mass of eulogy'. Perhaps this accounts for Wordsworth's coldness to Coleridge when they met in London in December 1817; for Coleridge had just published his *Biographia Literaria*, in which he disputed Wordsworth's 'peculiar tenets' about the language of poetry, and listed the defects of his poems as well as their excellencies. Among the former: inconstancy of style, and matter-of-factness; among the latter: austere purity of language, sinewy strength and originality, and above all imagination.

While in London, Wordsworth met Keats, then aged twenty-two, at the 'immortal dinner' given by Haydon the painter. Keats greatly admired Wordsworth's poetry, but was disappointed in the man: sorry that he 'left a bad impression wherever he visited in town by his egotism, Vanity, and bigotry'. They never met again, though Keats called at Rydal Mount in June 1818, on his way to Scotland.

Wordsworth was not at home; he was at Appleby, waiting for the results of the Westmorland Election.

The two county members for Westmorland were the Lowther brothers, sons of Lord Lonsdale, and supporters of the reactionary Tory Ministry of Lord Liverpool; and when, at the General Election of 1818, they were opposed by Henry Brougham, the Whig advocate of parliamentary reform, Wordsworth at once offered his services to the Lowther cause. As a young man he had protested that he was, and would always remain a democrat, but now he published an anonymous *Address to the Freeholders of Westmorland*, supporting the existing restriction of the franchise to owners of property. The surviving feudal power in England was a defence against the popular tendency to reform. The Lowther brothers won the election, and Keats wrote: 'Wordsworth versus Brougham! Sad – sad – sad!' And Shelley: 'What a beastly and pitiful wretch that Wordsworth!' Nevertheless, Wordsworth twice again helped the Lowthers to defeat Brougham.

In the following year, 1819, encouraged perhaps by Haydon's enormous painting of *Christ's Entry into Jerusalem*, in which he appeared as a spectator, he

'I hope your picture is not much hurt by my presence in it, though heaven knows that I feel I have little right to be there.'
Haydon's painting of *Christ's Entry into Jerusalem*, finished in 1819. Wordsworth, with bowed head, is in the opening on the right; beside him are Voltaire and Newton, and behind is Keats

published *Peter Bell*, the long narrative poem written at Alfoxden twenty years before. He must have known that this story of a potter and a donkey was an invitation to further ridicule, and that is what he got, including the satirical *Peter Bell the Third* from Shelley. He replied with a sonnet that told the 'harpy brood' how good the poem was (as indeed it was), and defiantly offered them another victim: *The Waggoner* of 1805, which received similar treatment.

Fortunately the sonnet sequence on the Duddon, the southward-flowing river first visited with Dorothy so many years before, was received with some enthusiasm when published in 1820. Here were no potters and pedlars, no donkeys and scenes from low life; both matter and manner were conventional, though there were lines,

Francis Chantrey's busts of Scott and Wordsworth (1820).

'I am happy my effigy is to go with that of W. for (differing from him in many points of taste) I do not know a man more to be venerated for uprightness of heart and loftiness of genius. Why he will sometimes choose to crawl upon all fours when God has given him so noble a countenance to lift to heaven I am as little able to account for as for his quarrelling with the wrinkles which time and meditation have stamped his brow withal.' Scott to Allan Cunningham

poems even, that recalled the earlier poet: the twenty-sixth – but that was based on an earlier version – and the last, addressed to Mary, with its memorable final line: 'We feel that we are greater than we know.'

The favourable reception of his sonnets seems to have had a mellowing effect on Wordsworth. He looked more than fifty, but after the harsh, disappointed decade of his forties, Robinson found him less opinionated and altogether more agreeable. It was just as well, for he joined him, with Mary and Dorothy, on a prolonged continental tour in 1820, when, to Dorothy's delight, they saw many of the places visited by her brother and Robert Jones thirty years before. In Lucerne they were seen by young Edward Trelawny: Wordsworth angular and bony,

Continental Tour

Christopher Wordsworth (1774–1846), William's youngest brother, Master of Trinity College, Cambridge, 1820–41.

His son Christopher, who became Bishop of Lincoln, wrote the first biography of his uncle: *Memoirs of William Wordsworth*, 1851

(*Opposite*) Wellington and Peel, who had ▶ opposed Catholic Emancipation, now lead its supporters, including Brougham, against its adversaries, 1829

self-confident and dogmatic, with peeling skin and harsh northern accent. He was complaining that one could no longer escape from travellers' carriages, even in the Alps, but when their carriage arrived, he called, 'Come lasses, be stirring . . . You may rejoice in not having to walk.' Trelawny plucked up courage to ask him what he thought of Shelley as a poet. 'Nothing,' he replied abruptly. Then, pointing to his Scotch terrier, he added, 'This hairy fellow is our flea-trap.' They stayed in Paris, where they saw Annette, Caroline and her two children, Wordsworth's granddaughters, and were back in England by November.

From London they went to Cambridge to stay with Wordsworth's only remaining brother, Christopher, recently elected Master of Trinity College. It was Wordsworth's first visit to his old university since he had taken his degree, and he was delighted to find his work appreciated by the undergraduates. They then went to Coleorton, where Sir George Beaumont was about to build a church, a project that prompted the writing of another sonnet sequence, *Ecclesiastical Sketches*. Catholic Emancipation was becoming an important issue, and this right of Catholics to sit in Parliament Wordsworth strongly opposed, as a threat to the Established Church. The *Sketches*, therefore, were both a history and defence of the Church of England, with the emphasis now on the Anglican Laud rather than the Puritan Milton. He had become an over-facile sonneteer, and most of the poems make dull reading, though they added to his reputation when published in 1822. The *Memorials of a Tour on the Continent* are equally uninspired. 'What a mighty genius is the Poet Wordsworth!' wrote his young friend and admirer Hartley Coleridge. 'What a dull proser is W. W. Esqre. of Rydal Mount, Distributor of Stamps and brother to the Revd. the Master of Trinity!'

Wordsworth wrote comparatively little during the remainder of the 1820s. After the fate of *The Excursion* he could not bring himself to continue *The Recluse*; a sonnet, 'a moment's monument', was much less fatiguing: almost like taking a snapshot. Then, the continental tour had made him restless. In 1823 he took Mary to Belgium and Holland, and in the next year Dora accompanied them on a visit to Robert Jones and North Wales.

Dora was now the beloved companion of Wordsworth, the fourth woman in the house to minister to his comfort, and in 1828, shortly before her twenty-fourth birthday, he and Coleridge took her for a holiday on the Rhine. In the following year he went to Ireland. It was the year of the Catholic Emancipation Act, followed by the fall of Wellington's Tory Ministry, the death of George IV, a General Election, and victory of the Whigs, pledged to reform, under Lord Grey. Wordsworth was full of foreboding; any change of the Constitution, he wrote to Lord Lonsdale, meant a violation of the existing order of society. He even opposed the foundation of a new University of London; Dissenters, virtually excluded from Oxford and Cambridge, would be admitted, and the place would be little more than a breeding-ground of revolutionary ideas. It must be remembered,

Dora

The Battle of the Petitions, a Farce now performing with great applause at both Houses.

Dorothy Wordsworth in 1833, aged 61. 'Her spirits, thank God, are good, and whenever she is able to read, she beguiles her time wonderfully . . . Her loving-kindness has no bounds.'
WW to Charles Lamb

Yarrow Revisited. Wordsworth and Scott at Newark Castle, 1831 ▶

Once more, by Newark's Castle-gate
Long left without a warder,
I stood, looked, listened, and with Thee,
Great Minstrel of the Border!

however, that he always retained his sympathy for Man, and, even while opposing the Reform Bill, wrote the lines *Humanity*, deploring the 'slavish toil' of factory workers in new industrial towns.

The decade of the 1820s had begun with the deaths of Keats and Shelley, followed by that of Byron in 1824. Byron had achieved international renown, and his meteoric brilliance had obscured the steadier glow of Wordsworth's genius; but after Byron's death, Wordsworth's reputation grew, until by 1830 the publication of collected editions of his works had established him as one of the leading poets of the century.

He suffered a severe personal loss in 1827, when his great friend and benefactor Sir George Beaumont died, and he commemorated this generous man in *Elegiac Musings*. The lines were composed after a visit to Coleorton, during a storm while he was riding Dora's pony from Lancaster to Cambridge on a visit to his brother.

His elder son John had been given a curacy near Coleorton, and it was while Dorothy was keeping house for him in 1829 that she was stricken with her first serious illness. She was fifty-seven, but still walked as she had walked with William and Coleridge in the old days, from Alfoxden to Stowey, from Grasmere to Keswick, and she appears to have overtaxed her strength. She recovered, but after her return to Rydal Mount, had another attack, which left her so weak that she had to resign herself to being an invalid confined to the house and garden.

Wordsworth at sixty was fit enough, apart from his eye-trouble, for which he sometimes wore a shade, and in September 1831 he took Dora to see Scott at Abbotsford. ' "There's a man wi' a veil, and a lass drivin'," exclaimed a little

Dorothy's illness

urchin, as we entered Merrie Carlisle,' he wrote, announcing his approach. Scott was partially paralyzed after a stroke, but was able to accompany them to the Braes of Yarrow. Wordsworth realized that this was probably the last time they would meet, and in *Yarrow Revisited* paid a moving tribute to the 'Great Minstrel of the Border'. Soon afterwards Scott sailed for Italy, and Wordsworth wrote a sonnet in which he sent him 'the whole world's good wishes'.

Scott, the most popular poet of the day, had written his last; Wordsworth was left with no real rival, and the year 1831 marks the beginning of widespread recognition. Artists now asked him for the honour of a sitting, and in July Dora wrote to a friend that one was painting him, another sketching him, a third moulding him for a bust. Earlier in the year the Fellows of St John's, his old college, had asked if they might commission a portrait, though it was September 1832 before Henry Pickersgill arrived at Rydal Mount. The delightful Dora was all excitement: 'Miss Hook and I, or "Hook and Eye" as we call ourselves . . . fairly quarrelled for Mr Pickersgill, alias "Pick", as I call him.' The portrait was exhibited in the Royal Academy, engravings were made from it, and henceforth Wordsworth was in constant demand as a subject.

While he was in Scotland the Reform Bill, passed by the Commons, had been thrown out by the Lords. There were riots, and the Bill was forced through Parliament only by the King's consent to create a sufficient number of Whig peers to carry it. Wordsworth deplored both the means and the end, the Act that reduced the power of great landowners like Lord Lonsdale, by extending the vote to the non-property-owning middle classes. In *The Warning* he gloomily prophesied old men desolate and streets full of outcasts and homeless orphans; he even thought of leaving the country to avoid the impending ruin.

Wordsworth in 1832, aged 62. 'Such a picture or rather head – for only the head is finished – he has made of Father! . . . None of the females of this house could gaze upon it for 5 minutes with eyes undimmed by tears.' Dora

The Reform Bill receives the King's assent, June 1832

'I have witnessed one revolution in a foreign country, and I have not courage to think of facing another in my own.' WW to CW, 1 April 1832

However, the Factory Act passed by the Reformed Parliament, giving some protection to children in cotton mills, was the kind of measure for which he had pleaded in *The Excursion*; but the new Poor Law, which ruthlessly forced the destitute into workhouses, children as well as adults, roused his indignation, as it did that of another great humanitarian, young Charles Dickens, whose *Oliver Twist* appeared soon afterwards.

These stormy years of strikes, riots, rick-burning, and near-revolution, which so frightened Wordsworth, were also a period of acute personal distress. One by one his great contemporaries were going. In 1832 Scott returned from Italy to die at his beloved Abbotsford. Coleridge followed in 1834. Their friendship had begun nearly forty years before, when the young man had come bounding over gate and field in his eagerness to reach Racedown; and although Wordsworth had seen little of him for the last twenty years, he always thought of him as the

Women working in factories: button making and mule spinning

'Miss Fenwick is more than a favourite with Mr and Mrs Wordsworth, and I do not think they can now live in perfect ease without her. No wonder; she is a *trump*.' Edward Quillinan

most wonderful man he had ever known. Lamb also died in 1834, and when James Hogg died a year later, Wordsworth was moved to write an elegy for all four. His late poetry was mainly perfunctory, written because it was expected of him, a habit rather than a compulsion, but in this lament for the makers, the poets, he wrote, almost for the last time, with the feeling and simplicity of his early days:

> *When first, descending from the moorlands,*
> *I saw the Stream of Yarrow glide*
> *Along a bare and open valley,*
> *The Ettrick Shepherd was my guide . . .*

In this year, 1835, his troubles rose to a climax. Mary's sister Sara, Coleridge's beloved Asra, who had lived with them for nearly thirty years, died in June. Then Dorothy had another of her attacks, and though she recovered, it was as a mentally deranged old woman who crouched over a fire all year long. Dora was another source of anxiety, not only on account of her delicate health, but also because she was in love with a man of whom Wordsworth, though he liked him personally, could not approve as a son-in-law: Edward Quillinan, an Irish Catholic, a widower, a half-pay captain of expensive tastes and no settled occupation. In 1835 Dora was thirty-one, but when she asked her father's consent to an engagement, he refused. No doubt he was thinking primarily of her happiness, but he could scarcely help thinking also of his own unhappiness if he lost yet *Isabella* another woman of his household. Fortunately he found another woman friend at *Fenwick* this critical time in Miss Isabella Fenwick; fortunately, too, for Dora, for it was she who persuaded Wordsworth to agree to the engagement.

'Dora was the joy and sunshine of their lives' ▶

In 1837 the young Queen Victoria succeeded to the throne, and Charles Darwin, back from his voyage to the Galapagos Islands, began to write the notes that were the germ of *The Origin of Species*. What Wordsworth would have thought of that epoch-making book we can well imagine; he mistrusted scientists, who 'murder to dissect' and 'break down all grandeur', and detested anything that might cast doubt on orthodox belief. But he did not live to read the book, and in March he and Crabb Robinson set off in a carriage for a five-month tour of Italy.

Italy with Crabb Robinson

In Paris he saw Caroline and her daughters. He was more interested in little girls and scenery, particularly waterfalls, than in ancient monuments, but in Rome he admired St Peter's, and dutifully inspected the Vatican sculptures, though in Florence he fell asleep before the Venus de Medici. They visited the Franciscan convent of Laverna, an excursion that occasioned a poem to the cuckoo that he heard there: once simply 'a wandering voice', but now 'the Voice of One Crying amid the Wilderness'. Its composition tired him; he was 'very uncomfortable' at Bologna, and the first sound of German speech, from the Austrians in occupation of Lombardy, roused his indignation, and the hope that Italy would soon be a united and independent nation.

They were in London again by the beginning of August: Wordsworth tired and homesick, glad to be back, Robinson, a bachelor, sorry their travels were over. He was only five years younger than Wordsworth, but was generally taken for his son, and enjoyed the things that Wordsworth abominated: gossiping and loitering in towns and taverns. Better still, however, he liked listening to Wordsworth, and in London recorded a conversation at the house of the wealthy, hospitable poet Samuel Rogers. 'He repeated emphatically that he did not expect, or desire, from posterity any other fame than . . . from the way in which his poems exhibit Man, in his essentially human character and relations – as child, parent, husband; the qualities which are common to all men, as opposed to those which distinguish one man from another.' Classical generalization rather than romantic differentiation.

◀ Coronation of Queen Victoria, 28 June 1838

An imaginary breakfast at Samuel Rogers': Rogers, Scott, Wordsworth, Southey, Coleridge

There was no need to wait for posterity; fame had come to him already. Rydal Mount was a centre of pilgrimage for inquisitive tourists, and there he entertained his friends; among them Dr Arnold, Headmaster of Rugby School, who bought a house in the neighbourhood. On his visits to London, generally in the spring of alternate years, he was lionized by the high society he had not long ago despised as incapable of appreciating his poetry; once at least he was cheered by the audience at Covent Garden Theatre. Then in 1838 came official recognition, when the new University of Durham awarded him the degree of Doctor of Civil Laws, an honour repeated a year later at Oxford, where he was greeted with 'thundering applause'.

In 1840 he was seventy, and there was little new poetry save occasional pieces. There was no Coleridge to encourage, or goad, him to continue *The Recluse*, so long postponed and now abandoned. He read little, partly owing to failing eyesight; instead, he dictated invaluable notes to Miss Fenwick, about when and how he wrote his poems; *Hart-Leap Well*, for example: 'Written at Town-End, Grasmere. The first eight stanzas were composed extempore one winter evening in the cottage. . . .' He also made a final revision of *The Prelude*. In his youth he had written in the hope of pleasing the young; now he was more concerned with the old. There are occasional felicities, as when he added the famous lines about Newton's statue:

> *The marble index of a mind for ever,*
> *Voyaging through strange seas of Thought, alone.*

Less felicitous was his revised reason for leaving France (and Annette) in 1792. In the original version it had been 'nothing else than absolute want of funds'.

(Opposite) Rydal Mount.
'This is master's *library*, but
he *studies* in the *fields*.'
A cookmaid

William and Mary
Wordsworth in 1839

Now he thankfully acknowledged that he had been 'Forced by the gracious
providence of Heaven'. All too often youthful passion is reduced to old-aged
prudence, an ardent pantheism to orthodox piety and moralizing in the manner of
The Excursion. We can see a similar process in one of the few good poems of his
last years. It begins with the simple clarity of his youth, though he would then
have claimed that flowers *are* conscious:

> *So fair, so sweet, withal so sensitive,*
> *Would that the little Flowers were born to live*
> *Conscious of half the pleasure which they give;*
>
> *That to this mountain-daisy's self were known*
> *The beauty of its star-shaped shadow, thrown*
> *On the smooth surface of this naked stone!*

Three comparable verses follow, but then the joy and colour fade into a grey moral.

Tennyson was 33 when Wordsworth, aged 72, met him. 'I hope he will live to give the world still better things'

He was also engaged with the publication of his work. His *Sonnets* – 415 of them – appeared in 1838, and after revising his early tragedy *The Borderers*, he published it in the volume of *Poems chiefly of Early and Late Years*. This was in 1842, the year in which he met young Tennyson, who had himself just published the poems that brought him fame, a fame that was soon to eclipse Wordsworth's for the remainder of the century.

Dora's Marriage   The decade of the 'Hungry Forties', of Chartism and railway mania, began with Dora's wedding. Wordsworth had at last given his consent, and in May 1841 she married Edward Quillinan at Bath, where Isabella Fenwick had a house. The service was conducted by Dora's elder brother John, now a Cumberland parson, and her younger brother William gave her away, for at the last moment, like Dorothy at his own wedding, Wordsworth felt unable to go to the church. Afterwards he and Mary and the others visited Alfoxden and Stowey, where his genius had first flowered. If he was deeply moved by these scenes of such happy memories of Dorothy and Coleridge, he did not betray his emotion: 'These were farewell visits for life, and, of course, not a little interesting.'

John and Dora were now provided for, but William was merely a Sub-Distributor of Stamps in his father's area. In 1842, therefore, Wordsworth went to London to arrange the transfer of his Distributorship to his son. This meant a loss of £400 a year, more than half his income, a sacrifice that he mentioned to Gladstone, who mentioned it to the Prime Minister, and in October Sir Robert Peel wrote to offer him a Civil List pension of £300 a year. He had reason to be satisfied with his London visit, for while he was there a Bill was introduced into Parliament to extend the period of copyright, a reform for which he had campaigned for some time. *The Prelude* would now bring in royalties for forty-two years from its publication after his death.

He still walked for at least two hours every day, and was a familiar sight to the countryfolk. 'You could tell fra the man's faace his potry would niver have no laugh in it.' 'I don't remember he ever laughed in his life, he'd smile times or two.' 'Never was heard to sing or whistle a tune in his life.' (He had no ear for music.) 'He wasn't a man as said a deal to common folk. But he talked a deal to hissen.' 'Would walk by you times enough wi'out sayin' owt, specially when he was i' study.' 'He was distant, ye may saay.' 'He was a lonely man.' Proud, shy, reserved, abstracted, yet 'He was a kind man, there's no two words about that: if anyone was sick i' the plaace, he wad be off to see til 'em.'

Striding Edge, Helvellyn. 'The lines [on a portrait of Wellington by Haydon] were composed while I was climbing Helvellyn. We had a glorious day, and Dora reached the top without ever dismounting. Mr Quillinan and I walked . . . I was seven hours on my feet without being at all tired.' 4 September 1840

He was kind to Southey, who had lived at Keswick for almost as long as he had lived at Grasmere and Rydal. At the height of his own troubles in 1835, he tried to comfort him and find a nurse for his wife, who had gone insane. Two years later she died, and Southey married again, but slowly declined into senility, fondling his beloved books like a child. He died at Greta Hall in March 1843, and Wordsworth was one of the few who attended his funeral in Crosthwaite church.

Poet-Laureate
A few days later he was offered the Laureateship. He refused on the ground of his 'advanced age', but when pressed by Peel, who assured him that no duties would be expected of him, he accepted. He even accepted an invitation to attend the Queen's Ball in 1845, when he appeared in a court dress borrowed from Samuel Rogers. 'It was a squeeze,' Haydon wrote in his diary; and then to Wordsworth: 'I wish you had not gone to court. Your climax was the shout of the Oxford Senate House. Why not rest on that? I think of you as Nature's high priest. I can't bear to associate a bag-wig and sword, ruffles and buckles, with Helvellyn and the mountain solitudes.' Haydon was painting Wordsworth's portrait 'on Helvellyn'.

Wordsworth now travelled by the new-fangled railway, liked it, and wrote a sonnet on *Steamboats, Viaducts and Railways*; but it was another matter when the

'I have accepted, with unqualified pleasure, a distinction sanctioned by her Majesty.' 4 April 1843

(*Above right*) The Queen's Fancy Dress Ball, 6 June 1845. 'A situation, I am not sorry to say, altogether new to me'

'I like railway travelling much.' Opening of the Stockton and Darlington Railway, 1825

'He would come often in the afternoon and have a talk at the Nab, and would go out with Hartley takin' him by t'arm.'
Wordsworth and Hartley Coleridge

railway threatened to invade his region of lakes and mountains. He wrote a very different sonnet on the proposed Kendal–Windermere line: 'Is then no nook of English ground secure / From rash assault?' The uneducated factory workers of Lancashire towns were incapable of appreciating mountain scenery, and should seek their recreation in more familiar country. If they arrived at Windermere in their thousands, they would only injure themselves, by driving away the wealthier inhabitants on whom they partly depended.

Dora's death   His attempt to repel the railway was interrupted by Dora's illness. In 1846, after a year in Portugal, she and her husband returned to the Lakes, where they took a house near Rydal Mount. That winter she went to Carlisle to prepare her brother William's house before his marriage. She was consumptive, caught cold, and on her return was moved to Rydal Mount to be nursed by her mother, but died in July 1847.

Wordsworth was plunged into a state of almost hopeless grief by the loss of his so dearly loved daughter. He sought comfort in the company of his sister Dorothy, beside the fire over which she huddled. But Mary was his support, the enduring wife and 'perfect woman' who had selflessly and unobtrusively looked after him for almost fifty years.

Then there was Coleridge's elder son, Hartley, who had inherited some of his father's genius and many of his infirmities. Wordsworth had been a second father to him, and for years had 'kep' li'le Hartley' near him at Nab Cottage. 'Li'le Hartley always had a bit of smile or twinkle in his face,' and in his company it was impossible not to forget sorrow for a time. But he died in 1849. 'Let him lie

Mary Wordsworth: 'A perfect Woman, nobly planned'

'A picture by Mr Haydon, representing me in the act of climbing Helvellyn.' 1842

Hartley Coleridge, 1796–1849

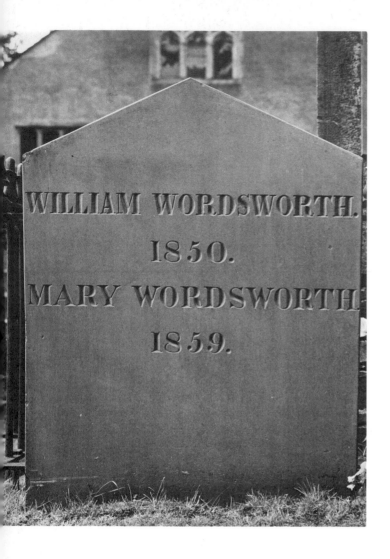

THE PRELUDE,

OR

GROWTH OF A POET'S MIND;

AN AUTOBIOGRAPHICAL POEM;

BY

WILLIAM WORDSWORTH.

LONDON:
EDWARD MOXON, DOVER STREET.
1850.

by us, he would have wished it,' said Wordsworth, and Hartley was buried among the family graves in Grasmere churchyard.

A year later Wordsworth caught a cold after going for a walk. It turned to pleurisy, and on 23 April, St George's and Shakespeare's Day, he died. He joined his three children in the churchyard, and a memorial was erected in Westminster Abbey. But Wordsworth's true memorial was *The Prelude*, the spiritual odyssey of the great poet who had died forty years before.

A SHORT BIBLIOGRAPHY

WORKS

The Poetical Works. The standard edition, ed. E. de Selincourt and H. Darbishire, 5 vols, 1940–49.

Lyrical Ballads. The editions of 1798 and 1800, ed. R. L. Brett and A. R. Jones, 1963.

Poems in Two Volumes. The edition of 1807, ed. H. Darbishire, 1952.

Poems of Wordsworth. A selection, ed. with a Preface by Matthew Arnold, 1879.

The Prelude, ed. E. de Selincourt, 1926. Revised H. Darbishire, 1959.

A Guide through the District of the Lakes, ed. E. de Selincourt, 1906.

LIFE AND CRITICISM

Letters of William and Dorothy Wordsworth, ed. E. de Selincourt, 6 vols, 1935–39.

Letters of William Wordsworth. A selection, ed. P. Wayne, 1954.

Some Letters of the Wordsworth Family, ed. L. N. Broughton, 1942.

The Journals of Dorothy Wordsworth, ed. E. de Selincourt, 2 vols, 1941.

Diary, Reminiscences and Correspondence of Henry Crabb Robinson, ed. T. Sadler, 3 vols, 1869.

Biographia Literaria. S. T. Coleridge: ed. J. Shawcross, 1907.

Lectures on the English Poets and *The Spirit of the Age.* W. Hazlitt. Everyman edition, 1910.

Memoirs of William Wordsworth. The first biography, by the poet's nephew, Christopher Wordsworth, 2 vols, 1851.

The Life of William Wordsworth. W. Knight, 3 vols, 1889.

William Wordsworth: A Biography. Mary Moorman, 2 vols, 1957, 1965. The standard biography.

William Wordsworth and Annette Vallon. E. Legouis, 1922.

The Age of Wordsworth. C. H. Herford, 1897.

Wordsworth. Walter Raleigh, 1903.

Wordsworth: Lectures and Essays. H. W. Garrod, 1923.

Wordsworth. Herbert Read, 1930, 1949.

Wordsworthian and Other Studies. E. de Selincourt, 1947.

The Poet Wordsworth. Helen Darbishire, 1950.

Wordsworth: A Re-Interpretation, F. W. Bateson, 1954.

William Wordsworth: The Prelude and Other Poems. J. F. Danby, 1963.

Portraits of Wordsworth. Frances Blanshard, 1959. The standard book on the subject.

Dorothy Wordsworth: A Biography. E. de Selincourt, 1933.

CHRONOLOGY

1770 7 April William Wordsworth born at Cockermouth, the second of five children.

1778 Death of his mother.

1779 School at Hawkshead.

1783 Death of his father.

1787 St John's College, Cambridge

1789 French Revolution begins.

1790 Walking-tour with Robert Jones: France, Switzerland, Italy.

1791 Stays in London.
December: goes to France.

1792 Meets Annette Vallon in Orléans. Michael Beaupuy converts him into a revolutionary republican.
October: goes to Paris.
December: returns to England, at about the time Annette gives birth to their daughter Caroline.

1793 February: France declares war on Britain. Publishes *An Evening Walk* and *Descriptive Sketches*.
Writes *A Letter to the Bishop of Llandaff*.

1794 Reunited with his sister Dorothy (b. 1771)

1795 Raisley Calvert leaves him £900. Goes to London, and meets William Godwin.
September: with Dorothy at Racedown Lodge, Dorset.

1796 Writes *The Borderers*.

1797 Writes *The Ruined Cottage*.
June: Coleridge visits Racedown. Wordsworth and Dorothy return with him to Nether Stowey.
July: with Dorothy rents Alfoxden House in the Quantocks.
November: genesis of *Lyrical Ballads*.

1798 A year of great creative activity.
Leaves Alfoxden, and tours Wye Valley with Dorothy. Writes *Tintern Abbey*.
September: with Dorothy to Goslar. Writes *Lucy* and *Mathew* poems, and begins *The Prelude*.
Lyrical Ballads published.

1799 May: Sockburn with the Hutchinsons. October: tours the Lakes with Coleridge.
December: settles at Town End (Dove Cottage), Grasmere, with Dorothy.

1800 Coleridge takes Greta Hall, Keswick. His brother John (b. 1772) stays at Dove Cottage.
Lyrical Ballads, in two volumes, published.

1802 Writes many poems, including *Immortality Ode*.
Lord Lonsdale pays debt owed to the Wordsworths.
August: with Dorothy goes to Calais to see Annette.
October: marries Mary Hutchinson at Brompton.

1803 First child, John, born.
The Southeys join the Coleridges at Greta Hall.

To Scotland with Dorothy and Coleridge. Meets Walter Scott.

1804 Coleridge goes to Malta.
Birth of his daughter Dora.

1805 February: his brother John drowned off Portland Bill.
October: Battle of Trafalgar.
The Prelude finished.

1806 Birth of his son Thomas.
Spends the winter with his family at Coleorton, where Coleridge joins them.

1807 *Poems in Two Volumes* published.

1808 Moves to Allan Bank.
Birth of his second daughter Catherine.
Convention of Cintra pamphlet.

1810 Birth of last child, William.
Quarrel with Coleridge.

1811 Moves to Grasmere Parsonage.

1812 Deaths of two of his children, Catherine and Thomas.

1813 Lord Lonsdale appoints him Distributor of Stamps for Westmorland.
Moves to Rydal Mount.

1814 Scottish tour with Mary. *Yarrow Visited.*
The Excursion published, and attacked by reviewers.

1815 Battle of Waterloo, and *Thanksgiving Ode.*

1816 His daughter Caroline (by Annette Vallon) married in Paris.

1817 Meets Keats in London.

1818 Westmorland Election: supports the Lowthers against Henry Brougham.

1819 *Peter Bell* and *The Waggoner* published.

1820 *River Duddon* sonnets published.
Continental tour with Mary, Dorothy, and Crabb Robinson.
Stays with his brother Christopher, Master of Trinity College, Cambridge.

1822 *Ecclesiastical Sketches* published.

1827 Death of his friend and patron Sir George Beaumont.

1830 Lord Grey's Whig Ministry.

1831 With Dora, visits Scott. *Yarrow Revisited.*

1832 Opposes the Reform Bill. Revises *The Prelude.*

1834 Death of Coleridge.

1835 Dorothy's mental breakdown.
Extempore Effusion upon the Death of James Hogg.

1837 Accession of Queen Victoria.
With Crabb Robinson to Italy.

1838–39 Awarded DCL degree by Universities of Durham and Oxford.

1841 Dora marries Edward Quillinan.

1842 Transfers Stamp Distributorship to his son William.
Awarded Civil List pension of £300 a year.
Poems . . . including The Borderers published.

1843 Appointed Poet Laureate after death of Southey.

1847 Death of Dora.

1850 23 April. Wordsworth dies.
The Prelude published.

NOTES ON THE PICTURES

Frontispiece: WILLIAM WORDSWORTH aged 74; oil painting by H. Inman, 1844. 'The best portrait that has been taken of the Poet – the Painter is an American.' M.W. 1844. University of Pennsylvania.

7 PENRITH: engraving by T.H. Fielding. From T.H. Fielding: *Cumberland, Westmorland and Lancashire Illustrated*, 1822. British Museum, Map Room.

8 WORDSWORTH'S BIRTHPLACE, Cockermouth. *Photo A. F. Kersting.*

9 JAMES LOWTHER, first Earl of Lonsdale; oil painting by T. Hudson, *c.* 1754. *By kind permission of the Earl of Lonsdale. Photo Abbot Hall Art Gallery, Kendal.*

11 COCKERMOUTH CASTLE; engraving by T.H. Fielding. From T.H. Fielding and J. Walton: *Picturesque Tour of the English Lakes*, 1821. Guildhall Library, London.

WHITEHAVEN; engraving by W. Daniell. From R. Ayton: *A Voyage round Great Britain*, 1814, Vol. II. Guildhall Library, London.

12 ESTHWAITE WATER, Lancashire, with the Westmorland mountains in the background. *Photo Barnaby's Picture Library.*

HAWKSHEAD GRAMMAR SCHOOL. *Photo Ian Yeomans; copyright 'Sunday Times'.*

13 ANNE TYSON'S COTTAGE, Colthouse. *Photo Ian Yeomans; copyright 'Sunday Times'.*

14 FURNESS ABBEY; engraving by T. Hearne (1744–1817) and W. Ellis (1747–1810) after T. Hearne and J. Farington (1747–1821). *Photo Courtauld Institute of Art, London.*

15 ROBERT BURNS; oil painting by A. Nasmyth (1758–1840). National Portrait Gallery, London.

16 A PAGE from an edition of Euclid's *Elements of Geometry* published in 1772.

17 BROUGHAM CASTLE from the north. From *Our English Lakes, Mountains, and Waterfalls, as seen by William Wordsworth*, 1864.

18 ENTRANCE TO ST JOHN'S COLLEGE, Cambridge; etching by Elizabeth Byrne after R.B. Harraden. From R.B. Harraden: *History of the University of Cambridge*, 1814, second edition.

ST JOHN'S COLLEGE, Cambridge, from Fisher's Lane; engraving by J.C. Stadler after W. Westall. From R. Ackermann: *A History of the University of Cambridge*, 1814.

19 THE ROOM IN ST JOHN'S COLLEGE, Cambridge, First Court, F2, occupied by Wordsworth 1787–91; drawing by R. Lofts, 1892. *By kind permission of The Master and Fellows of St John's College, Cambridge.*

SIR ISAAC NEWTON; marble statue by F. Roubillac, 1727. The Chapel, Trinity College, Cambridge. *Photo National Monuments Record. Crown copyright.*

20 DOVEDALE: engraving by J.C. Smith after E. Dayes, 1805. From E. Dayes: *A Picturesque Tour in Yorkshire and Derbyshire*, 1825.

21 A BLACK LEAD MINE in Cumberland; engraving by M. Prestel after P. de Loutherbourg, 1788–93. British Museum, Map Room.

22 FORNCETT ST PETER CHURCH AND RECTORY; lithograph by H. Ninham (1793–1874). City Museum, Norwich, R.J. Colman Todd Collection.

23 THE STORMING OF THE BASTILLE, 14 July 1789; engraving by J. Prieur. Louvre, Paris. *Photo Giraudon.*

FESTIVAL IN HONOUR OF THE FEDERATION, 18 July 1790: jousting on the Seine; engraving by P.G. Berthault after J. Prieur. From *Collections de Tableaux Historiques de la Révolution Française*, 1804, Vol. I.

24 THE GRANDE CHARTREUSE; watercolour signed 'AB', undated. British Museum, Map Room.

25 'THE MER DE GLACE, Chamonix with Blair's Hut'; pencil and watercolour over pencil on grey paper by J.M.W. Turner, 1802. British Museum, Department of Prints and Drawings.

'THE FALL OF THE RHINE at Schaffhausen'; oil painting by P. de Loutherbourg, c. 1775. Victoria and Albert Museum, London.

26 ANGLERS outside Sadler's Wells Theatre; watercolour by G. Cruikshank, 1796. Victoria and Albert Museum, London, Enthoven Collection.

MRS SIDDONS as Euphrasia in *The Grecian Daughter*; engraving by Caroline Watson after E. Pine, 1784. Victoria and Albert Museum, London, Enthoven Collection.

27 THE HOUSE OF COMMONS; oil painting by K. Hickel, 1793. National Portrait Gallery, London. W. Pitt is speaking, Addington in the chair and Fox in profile on the right.

29 SNOWDON; watercolour by J. Varley, 1800–10. Walker Art Gallery, Liverpool.

DIEPPE HARBOUR; watercolour by J. Crome, 1832. Victoria and Albert Museum, London.

30 ROULETTE GAME IN PARIS; anonymous watercolour, c. 1790. Bibliothèque Nationale, Paris.

'STREET SCENE in Paris with a group of Savoyards and their performing dogs'; pen, watercolour and gouache by C. Naudet, 1790. *Courtesy of the Ford Foundation.*

31 'THE REPENTANT MAGDALEN renouncing the vanities of the world'; oil painting by C. Le Brun (1619–90). Louvre, Paris. *Photo Giraudon.*

32 ORLEANS; engraving by L. Brion. From J. La Vallée: *Voyage dans les départements de la France*, 1792–93.

BLOIS, engraving by L. Brion. From J. La Vallée: *Voyage dans les départements de la France*, 1792–93.

33 ANNETTE VALLON; presumed miniature portrait. Frontispiece to E. Legouis: *William Wordsworth and Annette Vallon*, published by J.M. Dent and Sons Ltd, London, 1922.

(1781–1857). British Museum, Map Room.

55 SOCKBURN-ON-TEES farmhouse. *By kind permission of Professor Mary E. Burton.*

56 GRETA BRIDGE; watercolour by J. S. Cotman, 1810. Castle Museum, Norwich.

57 DOVE COTTAGE, Grasmere. *Photo Ian Yeomans; copyright 'Sunday Times'.*

58 FACSIMILE OF A PAGE from Dorothy Wordsworth's *Journal.* Wordsworth Museum, Grasmere.

INTERIOR OF DOVE COTTAGE, Grasmere. *Photo Ian Yeomans; copyright 'Sunday Times'.*

59 GRASMERE FROM RED BANK with Helm Crag and Dunmail Raise in the distance. From *Our English Lakes, Mountains, and Waterfalls, as seen by William Wordsworth,* 1864.

60 'THE EARL OF ABERGAVENNY, East Indiaman off Southsea'; oil painting by T. Luny, 1801. *Reproduced by courtesy of the Secretary of State for Foreign and Commonwealth Affairs.*

61 SARA COLERIDGE, wife of S. T. Coleridge; anonymous portrait. From R. Garnett and E. Gosse: *English Literature,* 1903.

GRETA HALL, Keswick.

63 THE INNOMINATE TARN, a lake at the top of the Haystacks Mountain near Buttermere. *Photo Barnaby's Picture Library.*

64 KESWICK LAKE. *Photo Edwin Smith.*

65 GRASMERE FROM LOUGHRIGG FELL; lithograph by T. Picken after J. B. Pyne. From J. B. Pyne: *Lake Scenery of England,* 1859.

67 'SARA'S ROCK'. *Photo Ian Yeomans; copyright 'Sunday Times'.*

68 THE ANTI-SLAVERY Society Convention; oil painting by B. R. Haydon, 1840. National Portrait Gallery, London.

69 ULLSWATER. *Photo G. P. Abraham.*

70 WESTMINSTER FROM THE SOUTH BANK; watercolour by F. Nicholson, 1790. Private Collection.

71 'CALAIS PIER: An English packet arriving'; oil painting by J. M. W. Turner, 1803. *Courtesy of the Trustees of the National Gallery, London.*

73 BROMPTON CHURCH. *Photo Ian Yeomans; copyright 'Sunday Times'.*

74 THE TOMB OF ROBERT BURNS, St Michael's Churchyard, Dumfries; aquatint by W. Bennett (1811–71) after M. A. Nicholson (1788–1833). Victoria and Albert Museum, London.

75 MELROSE ABBEY; watercolour by F. J. Sarjent, 1811. British Museum, Map Room.

76 GEORGE III reviewing volunteers, 4 June 1799; engraving by S. W. Reynolds after R. K. Porter, published 1800. British Museum, Department of Prints and Drawings.

'DIVERS PROJETS sur la descente en Angleterre'; anonymous undated engraving.

77 SKETCH FOR THE PAINTING *The Consecration of Napoleon,* 1805–07 by J.-L. David. Louvre, Paris.

Notes

THE ACTION OFF PULO A'OR, 15 February 1804; oil painting by T. Butterworth (*fl.* 1813–27). *Reproduced by courtesy of the Secretary of State for Foreign and Commonwealth Affairs.*

78 WEYMOUTH BAY; oil painting by J. Constable, undated. *Courtesy the Trustees of the National Gallery, London.*

79 LETTER FROM William Wordsworth to Richard Wordsworth, 11 February 1805. Wordsworth Museum, Grasmere.

THE DEATH OF NELSON; oil painting by D. Maclise, 1862–63. Walker Art Gallery, Liverpool.

80 MANUSCRIPT OF *The Prelude*, Book Thirteenth, with corrections by William Wordsworth. Wordsworth Museum, Grasmere. *Photo Ian Yeomans; copyright 'Sunday Times'.*

PIEL CASTLE IN A STORM; oil painting by Sir G. Beaumont, exhibited Royal Academy 1806. Leicester Museums and Art Gallery.

81 SIR GEORGE BEAUMONT; drawing by G. Dance, 1807. National Portrait Gallery, London.

WILLIAM WORDSWORTH; drawing by H. Edridge, *c.* 1806. Dove Cottage, Grasmere.

83 MANUSCRIPT OF A POEM by S.T. Coleridge to William Wordswoorth, *To a Gentleman*, January 1807. Wordsworth Museum, Grasmere.

COLEORTON HALL; oil painting by G. Arnald, 1811. *By kind permission of Sir George Beaumont.*

84 AN EXTRACT from *A Letter to Asra* in S.T. Coleridge's hand. Dove Cottage, Grasmere.

85 SARA HUTCHINSON aged about 42; anonymous silhouette. *By kind permission of Jonathan Wordsworth Esq.*

SAMUEL TAYLOR COLERIDGE; etching by L. Lowenstein (1842–98) after G. Dawe (1781–1829).

86 FRONTISPIECE TO *The White Doe of Rylstone*, 1815; engraving by J.C. Bromley after Sir G. Beaumont.

GORDALE. *Photo Edwin Smith.*

87 THOMAS DE QUINCEY; oil painting by J. Watson-Gordon, 1845. National Portrait Gallery, London.

88 SIR ARTHUR WELLESLEY'S quarters, Vimiero, 21 and 22 August 1808; engraving by J.C. Stadler after G. Landmann. From G. Landmann: *Historical, Military and Picturesque Observations on Portugal, 1818.*

89 THE THIRD OF MAY, 1808; oil painting by F. de Goya, 1814. Prado, Madrid. *Photo Mas.*

TITLE PAGE OF *Concerning the Relations of Great Britain, Spain, and Portugal to each other, and to the common enemy at this crisis; and specifically as affected by the Convention of Cintra*, 1809.

91 HENRY CRABB ROBINSON; drawing by J.J. Masquerier (1778–1855). Dr Williams's Library, London.

92 THE OLD RECTORY, Grasmere. Dove Cottage, Grasmere.

THE STAMP OFFICE, Ambleside; drawings by J. Harden (1772–1847). *In* the possession of A.S. Clay, Esq.

93 'A POET MOUNTED on the court Pegasus'; engraving published by J. Johnston, London, 1817. British Museum, Department of Prints and Drawings. Caricature of Southey as Poet Laureate.

94 INTERIOR OF THE SUMMER HOUSE at Rydal Mount. *Photo Ian Yeomans; copyright 'Sunday Times'*.

UPPER FALL, RYDAL. From *Our English Lakes, Mountains, and Waterfalls, as seen by William Wordsworth*, 1864.

95 RYDAL MOUNT. From *Our English Lakes, Mountains, and Waterfalls, as seen by William Wordsworth*, 1864.

96 ABBOTSFORD, home of Sir Walter Scott; engraving by J.B. Mould. From W. Deans: *Melrose and its environs*, 1834.

97 JAMES HOGG; watercolour by S.P. Denning (1795–1864). National Portrait Gallery, London.

'WALTER SCOTT and his friends at Abbotsford'; oil painting by T. Faed, 1849. Scottish National Portrait Gallery, Edinburgh.

98 THE SOLITARY'S COTTAGE, Blea Tarn; drawing by T.L. Aspland (1807–90). *By permission of the Trustees of the Armitt Library, Ambleside*.

99 WILLIAM WORDSWORTH, life mask by B.R. Haydon, 1815. National Portrait Gallery, London.

100 LOWTHER CASTLE, built 1810; engraving by J. Thomas after T. Allom. From T. Rose: *Westmorland, Cumberland, Durham and Northumberland Illustrated*, 1832.

101 WILLIAM WORDSWORTH; oil painting by R. Carruthers, 1817. *By kind permission of Jonathan Wordsworth Esq*.

102 THE BATTLE OF WATERLOO, 18 June 1815; oil painting by J.W. Pieneman. Rijksmuseum, Amsterdam.

103 THE PETERLOO MASSACRE, St Peter's Place, Manchester, 16 August 1819; anonymous undated engraving. Communist Party Library, London.

104 POSTER signed by H.C. Lowther thanking the people of Westmorland for their support at the Westmorland Election, 1818. Westmorland County Library, Kendal.

HENRY BROUGHAM, first Baron Brougham and Vaux; detail of oil painting by J. Lonsdale, 1821. National Portrait Gallery, London.

105 CHRIST'S ENTRY INTO JERUSALEM; oil painting by B.R. Haydon, 1819. St Gregory Seminary, Cincinnati, Ohio.

106 SIR WALTER SCOTT; marble bust by F. Chantrey, 1820. *By kind permission of Mrs Maxwell-Scott*.

107 WILLIAM WORDSWORTH; marble bust by F. Chantrey, 1820. Board of Trustees, Indiana University.

108 CHRISTOPHER WORDSWORTH (1774–1846), Master of Trinity College, Cambridge, 1820–41; oil painting by G. Robson, 1825. *By kind permission of the Master and Fellows of Trinity College, Cambridge*.

109 THE BATTLE OF THE PETITIONS; engraving published by J. Field, London, 1829. British Museum, Department of Prints and Drawings. Petitions for and

against Emancipation took up much time in the House of Commons 6 February–30 March and also in the House of Lords until 10 April. Defenders of the Constitution shown on the left, leader Eldon; attack led by Wellington.

110 DOROTHY WORDSWORTH; oil painting by S. Crosthwaite, 1833. Dove Cottage, Grasmere.

111 WILLIAM WORDSWORTH and Walter Scott at Newark Tower; lithograph by G. Cattermole (1800–68). *By kind permission of Mrs Mary Moorman.*

113 WILLIAM WORDSWORTH; oil painting by H. W. Pickersgill, 1832. *By kind permission of the Master and Fellows of St John's College, Cambridge.*

114 THE REFORM BILL receiving the King's assent by the Royal Commission, 7 June 1832 in the House of Lords; engraving by W. Walker after S. W. Reynolds, 1836. British Museum, Department of Prints and Drawings.

BUTTON MAKING, stamping, pressing and punching in Birmingham; anonymous lithograph. From C. Knight: *Cyclopaedia of the Industry of All Nations*, 1851.

115 MULE SPINNING; engraving by J. W. Lowry after T. Allom. From E. Baines: *History of the Cotton Manufacture in Great Britain*, 1835.

116 ISABELLA FENWICK; anonymous drawing. Dove Cottage, Grasmere.

117 DORA WORDSWORTH, wife of Edward Quillinan; watercolour on ivory by Margaret Gillies, 1839. Dove Cottage, Grasmere.

118 THE CORONATION of Queen Victoria, 28 June 1838; engraving by H. T. Ryall after G. Hayter, 1843. Victoria and Albert Museum, London.

119 BREAKFAST AT SAMUEL ROGERS'; engraving by C. Mottram (1807–76). Victoria and Albert Museum.

120 A ROOM AT RYDAL MOUNT; engraving by W. Westall, 1840.

121 WILLIAM AND MARY WORDSWORTH; watercolour on ivory by Margaret Gillies, 1839. Dove Cottage, Grasmere.

122 ALFRED TENNYSON; oil sketch by S. Laurence, c. 1837. City of Lincoln Libraries, Museums and Art Gallery. On loan to the National Portrait Gallery, London.

123 STRIDING EDGE, HELVELLYN. *Photo J. Allan Cash.*

124 ROYAL WARRANT appointing William Wordsworth Poet Laureate in succession to Southey, 1843. Dove Cottage, Grasmere.

125 THE FANCY DRESS BALL at Buckingham Palace, 6 June 1845; watercolour by L. Haghe, 1845. Royal Collection, Windsor Castle. *Reproduced by gracious permission of Her Majesty the Queen.*

THE OPENING of the Stockton and Darlington Railway, 1825; watercolour sketch by J. Dobbin (c. 1807–96). Science Museum, London.

126 WORDSWORTH and Hartley Coleridge at Rydal; watercolour sketch made from life by J. P. Mulcaster, 1844. *By kind permission of Mrs D. Mumford.*

127 MARY WORDSWORTH; watercolour on ivory by Margaret Gillies. Dove Cottage, Grasmere.

WILLIAM WORDSWORTH; oil painting by B. R. Haydon, 1842. National Portrait Gallery, London.

HARTLEY COLERIDGE; oil painting by R. Tyson, before mid-1846. University of Texas.

128 THE GRAVE of William and Mary Wordsworth, Grasmere. *Photo J. Allan Cash.*

TITLE-PAGE of *The Prelude*, 1850.

ABBREVIATIONS

INDEX

Numbers in italics refer to the illustrations